HEALTHY Home

*A Practical Guide to Build
a Spiritually Vibrant Family
. . . Starting with You*

Tim Alba

FaithHappenings Publishers

Denver, Colorado

Printed in the United States of America

Scripture quotations are from *The Holy Bible, New International Version NIV®*. Copyright © 1973, 1978, 1984, 2011 by Biblica, Inc.® Used by permission.

For bulk orders, please contact the author at:
TimAlbaWD@gmail.com

FaithHappenings Publishing
A division of WordServe Literary
700 Colorado Blvd. #318
Denver, CO 80206
admin@wordserveliterary.com

Cover Design: German Castro

Interior Book Design: Greg Johnson

Tim Alba (1962)

ISBN: 978-1-941555-62-0

First Printing 2026

To the people of Cross City Church

I love you.

I can never repay the prior generations of faithful leaders at Cross City who helped Anna and me raise kids that love Jesus. But I can try to help the next generation of families like mine.

I pray that God uses this book and study guide to strengthen your spiritual health and leave a family legacy of hearing Him say, "Well done, good and faithful servant!"

Godspeed!

Contents

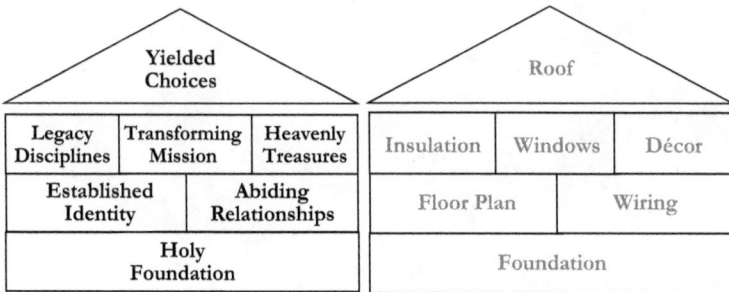

Yielded Choices			Roof		
Legacy Disciplines	Transforming Mission	Heavenly Treasures	Insulation	Windows	Décor
Established Identity		Abiding Relationships	Floor Plan		Wiring
Holy Foundation			Foundation		

Foreword

I love the title of Tim Alba's newest book, *HEALTHY Home*. More than just a great title, this book is an invaluable guide to help you build one—specifically, your own. If you are pursuing one of life's greatest callings—building a family—you will find this resource to be theologically sound, deeply practical, and thoroughly researched.

HEALTHY Home isn't just a book; it's a game plan. It will help you set clear goals, create alignment, call the plays, and navigate the often-underestimated challenges of family life.

As a pastor and father of six grown children (and now a grandfather), I'm acutely aware of how much our culture has changed—and how complex family life can be. People genuinely want to be spiritually healthy, but few know what that truly looks like. Yet amid those challenges, I've had the privilege of watching parents like Tim and Anna Alba build their homes with biblical wisdom, skill, and courage. And I love the results: strong, joyful, faithful children who have grown into spiritually healthy adults.

Tim and Anna are not just teachers—they're practitioners. I wouldn't want to read, much less endorse, a book on family life from someone who wasn't living it out. The Alba family radiates faith, fun, and authenticity.

When you read this book, you'll get a glimpse into their home and discover what Tim calls the "secret sauce" of building a spiritually vibrant family. You'll also see how you can use the "7 Big Rocks of a HEALTHY Home" to help your family *want what they need* to be faithful.

I've known Tim for more than twenty years—through his leadership in both the corporate C-suite and our church. He's authentic, practical, and thorough. He's taught this material to hundreds in our congregation and lived it out in countless conversations. Tim is consumed by a vision to see men and women rise up to build godly, healthy homes—and to one day hear God say, "Well done, good and faithful servant!"

We are leveraging this powerful content at our church through a sermon series, connection classes, and our practical mentoring ministry. I encourage you to use it too—with your family, your church, your mentees, or anyone who needs guidance on their spiritual journey. After all, as this book reminds us, "A healthy home starts with a healthy you."

Now you have the opportunity to benefit from that same passion and insight. My prayer is that *HEALTHY Home* will help you experience what God intends your home to be—a place of grace, growth, and generational impact.

John Meador
Lead Pastor, Cross City Church

Chapter 1

Choose a Family Spiritual Fitness Goal

Dream with me for a moment about your family.

If you could wish for one thing – anything – for your family, what would it be? Love? Safety? Success? Faith? Physical health? All good things that we all want.

For Christian families, though, there are three dreams – three spiritual fitness goals – that shape us. One of these three dreams is by far the most common. A second dream is shared by many Christians. But there's a third dream, a road less traveled, that changes everything when it shapes *your* family.

The first family dream is what everyone wants: a happy home.

Dream #1: Happy Home

How would you fill in this blank? "All I want is for my family to be ___." Inevitably, the answer I hear is "happy." Tired parents especially just want everyone to get along and be happy. It's the same with momma: If momma ain't happy, ain't nobody happy.

A happy home is great. But if your family dream is happiness, there's a problem. A big problem. If you're satisfied only as long as you get what you want, you might find happiness in the moment, but not the lasting joy you dream of.

Doing what you want in order to get what you want . . . that sounds so good, but it's no way to live. Happiness is so fleeting. Good luck keeping everyone in your family happy. You can't always know what they want because they often don't know what they want. And when they get what we want, they want something else. Happiness isn't a light switch that stays on; it's more like a blinking strobe light that drives you crazy because it's a fickle short-term goal with dangerous long-term consequences.

A happy home is better than an unhappy home, but there's something infinitely better that God wants for you and wants from you – the second family dream: a holy home.

Dream #2: Holy Home

I used to say that my goal as a parent was that my kids would be holy, not happy. I wanted both, but sometimes I had to choose between the two. And I chose holy. Because holiness brings happiness, but happiness doesn't bring holiness.

Holy cleans you up; happy just cheers you up. Holiness pursues God's will, not yours. God chose you to make you holy (Eph. 1:4) and declare you holy (1 Cor. 1:30), but you can never fully achieve holiness. You just receive it and pursue it.

Holy hearts are satisfied with less (Phil. 4:11-13) because they're satisfied with what they need, not what they want. And they know that God always provides what they need (Phil. 4:19).

A holy home is a great spiritual fitness goal because it's God's goal for you (1 Pet. 1:16, 1 Thess. 4:7). But holiness is often mistaken for three things: 1) just compliance, 2) just you and God, and 3) just emptying yourself of sin.

First, many people see holiness as just compliance (doing what you're required to do) instead of what you get to do. Holiness requires obedience. But obedience isn't begrudgingly complying with God's will; it's willingly aligning with God's will.

Second, while holiness is right-standing with God, it's not just you and God – secluded piety. Yes, you need daily God-and-me prayer time. Yes, you need to focus daily in His Word – the Bible – and let it guide every part of your life. But holiness isn't a lake that just receives; it's a flowing river that enlivens others, starting with your family. You can't make your family holy, but you can reflect the holiness of God that draw them in.

Third, although you (like all of us) can never be sin-free, you must continually empty yourself of sin. But just emptying yourself of sin isn't enough. Holiness is also being filled with the Holy Spirit. The amount of His filling you want, though, determines the amount of time you prepare. If you want a little holiness, you'll occasionally clean. But if you want a harvest of holiness, you'll keep sweeping, uncluttering, and making room for the Holy Spirit.

You can't do better than holy. However, there's a third dream that makes holy come alive with a vibrancy that attracts others to the faith that stirs your soul. This dream doesn't focus on just compliance, seclusion, and cleanliness. It turns spiritually flabby families into lean, mean spiritual machines. It's the third family dream: a spiritually healthy home.

Dream #3: Healthy Home

Every Christ-follower wants to be spiritually healthy, but many don't know what that looks like or where to start. After all, how can we pass down something we don't understand and can't describe?

Spiritual health, like physical health, has two parts. Physical health is: 1) the absence of illness and 2) complete well-being. Not one. Both. You can't be physically healthy with the existence of illness. But being free from illness doesn't mean you're healthy and strong. You're just not sick.

The same is true of spiritual health, which also has two parts: 1) the absence of ongoing sin and 2) complete faithfulness. Both are needed. And as we'll see in later chapters, both flow from the source of spiritual health – wanting what you need to be faithful.

God won't affirm ongoing, unconfessed sin, no matter how well intended it may be. But just avoiding the "worst" sins doesn't make you spiritually healthy and strong. You can be clean yet empty, like the man in Luke 11:24-26 who got cleansed of a demon but became worse off when seven demons returned. Why? Because, like many Christian homes, he was clean of what's wrong but not filled with what's right. Free from the presence of demons but not filled with the presence of God. Still susceptible, due to a lack of spiritual well-being. And so are we if we don't do both – root out sin and fill the void with complete faithfulness.

A healthy home is vibrant because it's both free from bondage and free to live victoriously. It hates sin and savors the Savior. It rejects an old sin nature and revels in a new Christ nature. It engages and builds up. It energizes and activates you to be strong and steadfast in your walk with Him. It strives for exceedingly abundant life on earth and eternal life in heaven (1 Tim. 4:8).

Spiritual health doesn't lay a new foundation; it builds on Christ's foundation (1 Cor. 3:11-13). It's the pursuit of "wholly holy" – a holiness that fills and fulfills the whole you. Being wholly holy strengthens. It sticks. It satisfies. And it saturates your family because you're instilling faithfulness from within them, not trying to install faithfulness upon them.

A healthy home, though, isn't just a dream. It can be a vivid reality by taking steps to turn good works into the fruit of the Spirit – happiness into joy, friendship into love, pleasure into peace, doggedness into patience, tolerance into kindness and goodness, good intentions into faithfulness, empathy into gentleness, and self-awareness into self-control (Gal. 5:22-23). And where does a healthy home start? It starts with a healthy you.

A Healthy Home Starts with a Healthy You

If you want your home to be healthy, *you* need to be healthy. Your faithfulness won't guarantee theirs, but it's the biggest factor in what they choose. Kids grow up thinking that your spiritual health

– good or bad – is normal. For example, my young kids assumed that all dads were impatient because I struggled with patience. But they also assumed it's normal for a dad to love his wife, a wife to respect her husband, and grandparents to selflessly serve people in need. And although they said we were "SO boring!", they eventually realized that our boring family wasn't so bad after all.

Years later, though, I realized that I was making a common mistake – I was trying to create little copies of me, instead of little copies of God. Indeed, you can have good intentions and good works, yet still miss the mark.

While your family needs to see God's Spirit thriving in you, they also need you to help them pick their own spiritual fitness goal and walk their own path to faithfulness. And a great place to start is dreaming big and aiming small.

Dream Big

Having no dream is dangerous, as is dreaming about things that don't matter. But an even stealthier danger is dreaming small. Whether it's fear, fatigue, failures, or something else, your family needs you to overcome any excuses for not dreaming big.

Set a high bar. Ask God to do great things through your family. You're created in His image, so dream like it. Yes, we need balance. But it's better to burn out while pursuing a grand goal than rust out with mediocre dreams. Dreaming big isn't reckless; it's world changing when we're preparing our family to be faithful.

In my book *Well Done, Mom & Dad!*, I share three core needs – vision, character, and culture – to prepare your family to be faithful. But it starts with a vision, a grand dream, of what God wants for your family and how to turn what is into what can be.

For decades my personal dream was to hear Jesus say, "Well done, good and faithful servant" (Matt. 25:21). I talked about my personal dream often, created a family mission statement based on it, and even commissioned a painting to visualize it. And although my fervor to hear "Well done!" hasn't waned, God did a fresh work in me. He gave me a new dream, a *family dream*, that absolutely grips my soul – the dream of watching Jesus do the same thing . . . with my kids and grandkids!

Personal dreams are great, especially if they're God-honoring and clear. But a family dream dares to dream bigger, lead bolder, and serve better. It promises more. And it requires more. We must become a better student of God as well as a better student of each family member's needs and gifts in order to bond each of them to God. A family dream is harder than a personal dream, but it's much, much grander. And that's the point!

A big family dream also encourages and challenges you, no matter how your family responds. When my family did various exercises to unpack and apply our family dream, my kids gave me eye rolls, slumped shoulders, and heavy sighs. But when my kids became adults, I learned how those exercises had helped shape their own God-sized dreams and led them to the second part of knowing where to start: Aim small.

Aim Small

When marksmen aim small, one of two things happen. They either hit the bullseye or they miss small. In the movie *The Patriot*, the lead character saves his son from certain death by urging his fellow shooter to "Aim small. Miss small." By aiming small, even when you miss the bullseye (and we all miss it sometimes), you'll still hit a worthwhile target.

So, the question is: What should you aim for?

The answer: Aim only at what you need to hit.

Don't aim at things that don't matter. For example, as a young parent, I fought every little battle. And while it's true that faithfulness in little things enables faithfulness in big things, it's also true that I harped on too many little things. I had to learn that aiming small isn't focusing on small things; it's focusing on the heart of big things with direction, determination, and devotion.

First, aiming small requires direction. What are you aiming for? Early on, I was so busy, tired, and distracted with providing for my family that I didn't always aim at what they needed. Sound familiar? It's so easy to get "directionally challenged" unless we let the Bible and the Holy Spirit point us in the right direction.

The aim of my church, Cross City Church, is to be real people with real hope and experience real life in Jesus Christ. We define REAL as: Relate well to God and people; Engage people with the gospel of Jesus Christ; Adopt them into the body of Christ; and Lead them to be Christ-followers. REAL isn't a motto; it's our aim. And while you don't need an acrostic, you need an aim. Do you and your family know what you're aiming for?

Second, aiming small requires a determination to keep your target in the crosshairs. And that involves doing things you dislike or aren't good at. But what's worse than doing unpleasant, important things is the regret of not doing them. Therefore, this book takes aim at four questions that we all need to answer but likely don't get around to considering:

What's my family's dream?	(Chapter 1)
Where are we in realizing this dream?	(Chapter 2)
How can this dream become a reality?	(Chapters 3–10)
How can we keep living this dream?	(Chapters 11-12)

And third, aiming small requires devotion to the people you love. They're real people in need of real hope and real life. They're counting on you. And they need you to stay devoted to the daily choices that help them be faithful.

Who's counting on you to dream big and aim small?

Here's the family that keeps my dream big and my aim small (plus three grandkids not yet born then).

7

How big is your dream?
How small is your aim?

Even if you're not yet confident in your aim, take a shot. Your family will understand misfires, but what they won't forgive is not trying. You can always reload and re-aim. Just make sure your family's spiritual fitness goal is a vibrant, healthy home. If so, strap on . . . this is about to get really good!

To get started, the next chapter provides a simple tool – a "spiritual stress test." It takes only 15 minutes to complete, but it can change your life. As I jokingly tell our HEALTHY Home classes, these 15 minutes can save you 15 years of counseling. Granted, great Christian counseling is a powerful tool to strengthen and heal families, but why not build an immunity to stop the endless cycle of spiritual pain and recovery?

By taking this assessment, you'll be on your way to knowing the spiritual health of you and your family. And once you know your spiritual condition, you can improve it.

Chapter 2

Take a Spiritual Stress Test

Who loves going to the doctor? Nobody. But if I want to be physically healthy, I need an assessment of where I am physically. And if I want to be spiritually healthy, I need to know where I am spiritually. I can't help my family get where we need to go if I don't know where we are.

Therefore, after deciding where you want to go (your family's spiritual fitness goal in Chapter 1), this chapter provides a self-assessment tool – a spiritual stress test – to highlight spiritual strengths and weaknesses. It's called the HEALTHY Home Wheel based on the "7 Big Rocks" of spiritual health.

Like great ancient buildings, great families are built with big rocks. Once these big rocks are secure, you can build everything else around them. Stephen Covey illustrates this with three bowls. One bowl is empty, one has little "unimportant" rocks, and one has big "important" rocks. If you pour all the little rocks into the empty bowl and then add the big rocks, the big rocks don't all fit.

But they all fit if you start with big rocks and fill in the gaps with little rocks. And even if some little rocks don't fit, it doesn't matter because the big rocks get in. Similarly, we need to fill our lives and families first with these 7 Big Rocks of spiritual health.

Doing this, though, is hard. It's easier to fill your life with little rocks, even though they don't accomplish much or keep you out of a spiritual ditch. Granted, if you're in a ditch you need to get out, but getting in and out of ditches is no way to live. Instead, fill your family with the big rocks that keep you from being ditch dwellers. Later, we'll unpack the 7 Big Rocks (the first letters of which form the acrostic HEALTHY), but here they are:

H – Holy foundation
E – Established identity
A – Abiding relationships
L – Legacy disciplines
T – Transforming mission
H – Heavenly treasures
Y – Yielded choices

Our spiritual stress test begins with these seven statements that summarize the 7 Big Rocks of spiritual health:

Holy foundation:	**My foundation is firm and biblically based.**
Established identity:	**My identity aligns with God's identity for me.**
Abiding relationships:	**My relationships reflect God's abiding love.**
Legacy disciplines:	**My daily disciplines create a godly legacy.**
Transforming mission:	**My mission transforms everything in my life.**
Heavenly treasures:	**I am laying up treasures to give Jesus in heaven.**
Yielded choices:	**I allow God to control my daily choices.**

In a moment, you'll score your spiritual health. That is, on a scale of 1 (low) to 10 (high), how much do you agree with the above seven statements? But let's first show how this assessment works for someone named Alicia with these seven scores:

<u>Alicia's scores:</u>

H – Holy foundation:	7		T – Transforming mission:	4
E – Established identity:	6		H – Heavenly treasures:	6
A – Abiding relationships:	8		Y – Yielded choices:	4
L – Legacy disciplines:	5			

Starting with the H – Holy foundation section (top right), Alicia marks the 7th ring of the wheel below because her score is 7 for that big rock. Moving clockwise, she marks the 6th ring of the E – Established identity section due to a score of 6, and so on for each big rock. When she's done, Alicia's wheel looks like this:

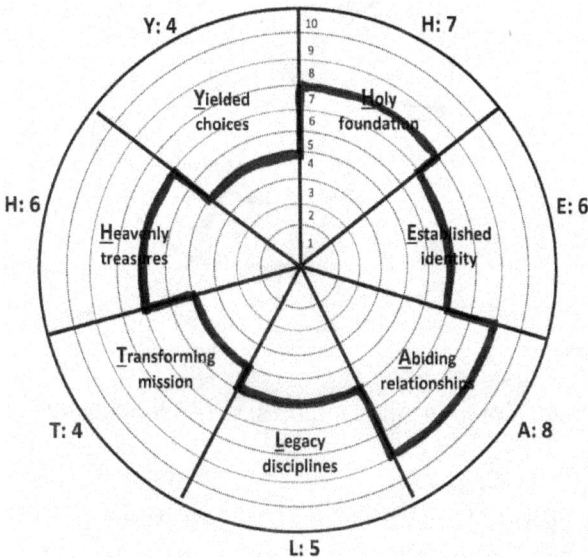

Next, you'll score the health of *your home*. Although each family member's score may be different, you'll write one score for how much the above 7 Big Rock statements reflect the overall spiritual health of your immediate family.

For your home's scores, you'll use a dashed line to distinguish it from your own scores. For example, by adding Alicia's home scores (as shown below), here's what her wheel looks like for herself (solid line) and her home (dashed lines).

Alicia's home scores:

H – Holy foundation:	6	T – Transforming mission:	2
E – Established identity:	2	H – Heavenly treasures:	3
A – Abiding relationships:	7	Y – Yielded choices:	3
L – Legacy disciplines:	3		

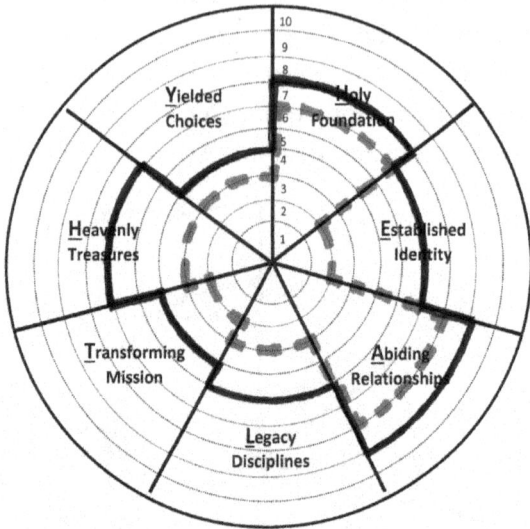

If you colored in Alicia's scores, they'd look like this.

Alicia's spiritual health

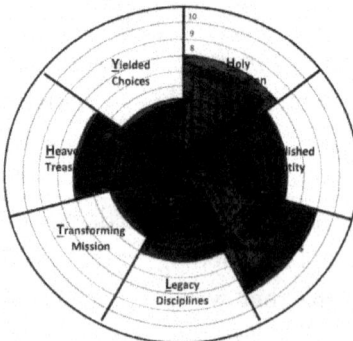

Alicia's home's spiritual health

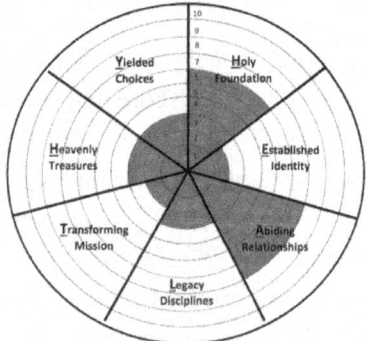

Alicia's own scores (solid lines) show a strong holy foundation and abiding relationships. But she lacks yielded choices, a transforming mission, and legacy disciplines. Alicia's struggles also affect her home, whose wheel (dashed lines) is smaller and wobblier than hers, especially with their identity and mission.

Now it's your turn. On a scale of 1 (low) to 10 (high), score the spiritual health of you ("You" column) and your home ("Home" column) based on how much you agree with the prior seven statements of the 7 Big Rocks.

	You	Home
H – Holy foundation	——	——
E – Established identity	——	——
A – Abiding relationships	——	——
L – Legacy disciplines	——	——
T – Transforming mission	——	——
H – Heavenly treasures	——	——
Y – Yielded choices	——	——

Using a black pen, mark your own scores with a solid line. And with a red pen, mark your home's scores with a dashed line.

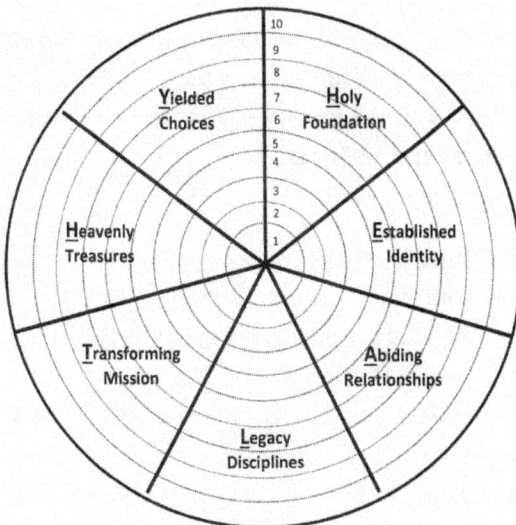

The size and wobble of your wheel are so important because they reflect the strength and consistency of your spiritual life. What does this initial assessment say about your spiritual health? Your family's spiritual health? How wobbly are your wheels? How big are they? What areas are the strongest? Which ones need the most improvement?

After exploring the 7 Big Rocks in coming chapters, you'll redo the HEALTHY Home Wheel. But as you consider them, here are three principles to help you take next steps.

1. Know your wobble

We all wobble. We all get out of balance. Life's hazards, obstacles, and normal wear and tear cause us to leak a little of God's filling. We also wobble when we get an inflated or deflated view of ourselves. The problem isn't that we get flat; it's that we stay flat, oftentimes without knowing why. Therefore, we'll explore why you and your family have had a bumpy life.

2. Smooth your wobble

The bumpier your spiritual life gets, the harder it is on your family. The goal isn't to skyrocket from a 2 to a 10; it's to turn a 2 into a 3, and then a 4, and so on – to take next steps that smooth your wobble. And while we want smooth paths and a spotlight to make it obvious, God wants something better for our journey. He wants us to trust Him and trust His Word to be a lamp and a light to guide our next steps (Ps. 119:105).

3. Worsen your wobble

Yes, making your wobble worse is counter intuitive. And, yes, if one of your big rocks is significantly lower than the others, you need to improve it. But if a big rock is just slightly lower, don't obsess with it. Instead, maximize your strengths. And even though it will cause you to be a bit wobbly, the goal isn't a perfectly smooth ride. The goal is a spiritually healthy home.

The side effect of being preoccupied with weaknesses is that it limits faithfulness. Fixing them won't make you great because major weaknesses rarely become major strengths. Fix weaknesses, but don't fixate on them. Instead, improve weaknesses to the point that they stop negating your strengths. Then use the 80/20 rule. Spend 20% of your time improving weaknesses and the remaining 80% maximizing strengths.

Lasting spiritual legacies are forged by a combination of no glaring weaknesses and at least one phenomenal strength. How has God gifted you to be phenomenal and make a powerful impact? How can you maximize those strengths for God's glory?

A great place to start is having each family member complete the HEALTHY Home Wheel for them and your family. This gets everyone on the same page and using a common language. It reveals how everyone views their own spiritual health and the health of your family. And it helps create a willingness to learn how they can build up each other into separate, yet connected, pieces of a spiritually healthy home.

When asked about how old kids should be to take this spiritual stress test, my answer is what I call the Disney World dilemma. That is, how old should your kids be when you take them to Disney World? When my daughter competed in a national jump rope tournament at Disney, her brother, Caleb, was only five years old. He had fun, but he didn't fully grasp the experience. Still, I'm glad we went because we experienced it together as a family.

So too, I encourage families to take this spiritual stress test as early as possible because it can help you build a culture of spiritual health. Your kids may not fully grasp it, but if they can engage in follow-up conversations, it's time to start. You'll decide when they're ready, but if they're preteens, they're likely ready. And if they're teenagers or older, they're definitely ready. Yes, they may balk. My kids balked too when we did spiritual assessments and exercises together, but years later they thanked me. Kids are more ready to engage in spiritual matters than we think they are.

No matter when you start (or re-start) your journey to spiritual health, please do it together as a family. The lessons you'll learn will be helpful, but the memories you make together will last a lifetime. And although they won't remember all the details, they'll never forget the journey of becoming "living stones (that) are being built into a spiritual house" (2 Pet. 2:5).

As we'll see beginning in the next chapter, you can turn that dream into a reality by building a HEALTHY home.

Chapter 3

Build a HEALTHY Home

Physical health. Everyone wants it, but what is it? Sure, I need to eat better and exercise more, but how exactly? What daily disciplines do I need? Where do I start? And how can I be physically healthy if I don't know clearly what it is?

So too, how can you be spiritually healthy if you can't describe it or know how to get there? What foundation should you build? What habits should you practice? What truths should you apply? Turns out, we don't need new truths. We just need to live out the timeless truth of Jesus' sermon on the mount: to be salt and light, pure, forgiving, loving, giving, praying, and storing up heavenly treasures (Matt. 5-7). Jesus then concludes his sermon with how building spiritual health is like building a *successful house*:

> "Everyone who hears these words of mine and puts them into practice is like a wise man who built his house on the rock. The rain came down, the streams rose, and the winds blew and beat against that house; yet it did not fall, because it had its foundation on the rock. But everyone who hears these words of mine and does not put them into practice is like a foolish man who built his house on sand. The rain came down, the streams rose, and the winds blew and beat against that house, and it fell with a great crash." (Matt. 7:24-27)

A Successful House

While houses share common characteristics, each house is unique and special. To be successful, a house must be designed, built, and managed well. And as we'll see in later chapters, a house needs seven sequential steps. The design might vary, but each of these seven steps is crucial for its success:

1) Build the right **Foundation**
2) Frame it by following the **Floor Plan**
3) Connect it to the power source with **Wiring**
4) Protect it with plenty of **Insulation**
5) Enlighten it with **Windows**
6) Fill it with timeless **Décor**
7) Inspect it for a compromised **Roof**

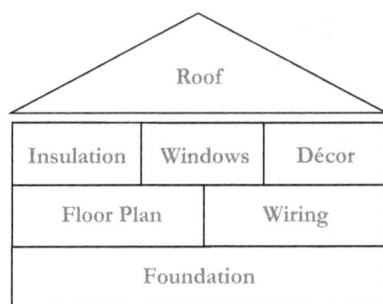

A Spiritually Healthy Home

We also want a successful family, but success isn't the goal. As stewards of our family's eternity, our goal should be a vibrant spiritual health that answers these seven questions:

1) Who is God?
2) Who does God say I am?
3) How can I connect with God and people?
4) How can I build a legacy that lasts?
5) What is my mission and how can I fulfill it?
6) How can I lay up treasures in heaven?
7) How can I actually do this?

The next seven chapters answer these questions by showing how the 7 Big Rocks of a HEALTHY home align with the seven steps of a successful house. And when we're done, our home and our house will look like this:

Yielded Choices			Roof		
Legacy Disciplines	Transforming Mission	Heavenly Treasures	Insulation	Windows	Décor
Established Identity		Abiding Relationships	Floor Plan		Wiring
Holy Foundation			Foundation		

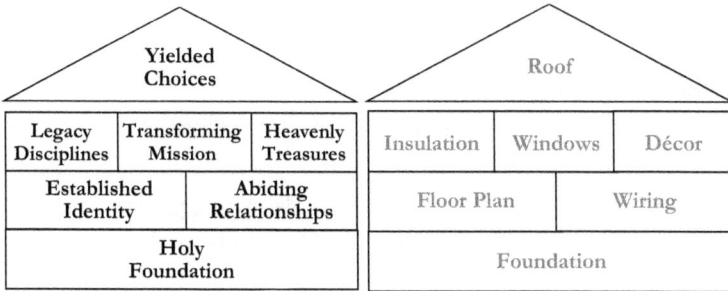

But before we explore how to build a spiritually healthy home, we need to consider its three components:

1. help your family want
2. what they need
3. to be faithful

1. Help your family *WANT*

Healthy homes create a desperation – a want-to – for the things of God, not just things you want or things they want.

You can beg, bribe, and threaten your little princess to go potty. But until she has a want-to, it's not happening. So too, spiritual health must be what she wants for herself, not just what you want for her. For spiritual health to stick for her, it must click for her. So, let's break this want-to into three smaller parts.

• First, healthy homes *help*.

Healthy homes help by being kind without coddling. They help you set expectations without controlling or commanding. They dream with you without choosing for you, and they come alongside you instead of pushing or dragging you. They facilitate, guide, and support you to help you choose well.

- Second, healthy homes know your audience – *your family*.

Other than God, your main audience is your family. Not you. Not your career. Not your church. Not your finances. Not your friends. Your family is your #1 ministry. For example, when my former pastor was a kid, his dad (who also was a pastor) took him to the circus instead of visiting an ill church member. His dad sacrificed a lot for his church, but he would not sacrifice his family. He had promised to take them to the circus, so he did, despite the ill member getting mad. And by doing so, he built a want-to in his son, who two decades later became my pastor.

- And third, healthy homes prepare you to *want*.

Healthy homes prepare you to *want* to choose well. This isn't a dictate. Not just a willingness or acceptance. It's a desperation mined from deep inside you. Then again, how do you feel when you're told what to do? Even if it's good for you, you'll balk, right? But when you're led to want it, all you need is guidance and encouragement to stay the course.

Over the years, I've seen two kinds of young families at church on Sunday. One family brings their kids; the other drags their kids. The first family is comfortable at church because God is comfortable in their home; the second squawks on Sundays because they expect the church to do what they don't do at home.

A great church can't take your place, but my faither-in-law was right when he said, "Tim, pick a church that helps you raise your family and stay there!" And that's a huge part of why we've stayed at Cross City Church for four decades – because they help families build a holy desperation (a want-to) for the second component of spiritual health: what they need (a need-to).

2. *What they NEED*

Healthy homes create a determination – a need-to – for what they need, not what you need or what they think they need.

I'll never forget the hipster salesman who insisted I buy eyeglasses like his. If he had bothered to read the room at all, he could tell I didn't want his funky frames. Instead of asking about my wants or needs, he pushed me to what he thought I needed. But, hey, I do the same thing sometimes. Especially as a young spouse, parent, and boss, I tried to get others to want what I wanted or needed, not what they needed.

Knowing what your family needs is hard because each person is unique and their needs change. Plus, they likely don't know what they need either. So, how can you know? Here are three questions to help you discern wants versus true needs.

- How are they wired? I had my kids take spiritual gift tests and personality tests. And I had a consultant assess one of my kids' giftedness. Why? Because you can't pursue what you need if you don't understand what you need.

- Can they distinguish between wants and needs? If not, they can't prioritize big rocks from little rocks.

- Do their perceived needs align with biblical principles and God's character? If not, they're wants, not needs.

For clarity, I wanted my kids to get what they wanted too, because I wanted them to be happy. But there's a long list of things they want, and only a few things they truly need. For example, my son somehow had a knack for dating models. After one dating disaster ended, I said, "Caleb, you need to decide what you need in a girl, and it needs to be a very short list. Not things like how she looks. And one of those few things you need is a girl who thinks deep like you." Why? Because he needs someone to connect deeply with him. (And, yep, Caleb found Emily, his beautiful, deep-thinking bride.)

Another example was my father-in-law, who used to say, "I need some Doritos." While he didn't mean it because he knew he didn't *need* Doritos, that kind of statement can be dangerous if your family doesn't learn the joy of sacrificing their wants for their needs. Learning this joy, though, births an even greater joy – the joy of sacrificing their wants for someone else's needs because it builds a determination for the third component of spiritual health – a destination of faithfulness.

3. *To be FAITHFUL*

Healthy homes create a focus and a passion – an I-will-do – for the one thing we all need: to be faithful.

I've failed if I don't make it easy for my family to be faithful. Notice, I didn't say that I've failed if my family isn't faithful, because I can't make their choices. But I can prepare them to want to be faithful based on how well I submit, serve, and lead.

I also must help them know who decides if they're faithful. God decides. Not them. Not you. God alone knows if they're desperate and determined to have a home built on faithfulness. And that doesn't happen by default. It takes a want-to, a need-to, and an I-will-do, which come from living these three truths:

- Your needs are greater than my wants. So, I submit.
- Your needs are greater than your wants. So, I serve.
- What you need most is to be faithful. So, I lead.

Does your family want what they need to be faithful? The next seven chapters can help you turn that dream into a reality. But let's first clarify this book's purpose. It's neither a quick-fix formula nor an exhaustive study. This book is a practical guide with a framework to help you build a spiritually healthy home, based on the book of Ephesians. It provides truths to apply, Bible verses to personalize, simple exercises to practice, and questions to discuss so that you'll walk worthy of your calling – to equip and build up your family into mature Christ-followers (Eph. 4:1,12-13).

But please remember . . . your faithfulness isn't based on your family's spiritual health. Your faithfulness is based on how well you prepare your family to be spiritually healthy. And that's never truer than what you do when you mess up.

When You Mess Up

The question isn't *if* you mess up; it's what you learn when you do. My family and I miss the mark sometimes too. Here are a few of our less-than-stellar moments, which might just make you feel a little better about yourself:

- As a young husband, I had a hilarious idea – to give Anna a mid-year evaluation. Let that sink in, and then forgive me because she did. Although I thought it would be funny, Anna thought otherwise. And, no, I never tried that one again.

- I once blurted out: "Hey, kids, Mom's on a diet. She's eating with only one hand." Oh, so wrong! Although Anna is gorgeous, it didn't matter. #stupidstupidman.

- I got home after a frustrating workday and, without thinking, began barking orders. Anna's retort: "The kids and I are NOT your employees!" Wow, that wake-up call changed my life.

- At a movie theater, my young son read a sign out loud: "No outside food allowed." Then he said, "Mom, is it a sin to bring snacks to the movies?" Anna's reply, "Well, it's a SIN what they charge for snacks!" While that's out of character for Anna, we all have those moments.

- After months of failed potty training, Josh yet again pooped his pants. In total frustration, Anna took him to the back yard, stripped him naked, and blasted him with a water hose. Unfazed, Josh hiked up his little hiney and proudly proclaimed, "You missed a spot!"

Like you, my family messes up too. But a healthy home isn't a perfect home. When healthy homes mess up, they fess up, forgive, and forge ahead. They learn and grow. They still love each other. And they make it easy for each other to want what they need to be faithful.

And that starts with the first big rock of a HEALTHY home: H – Holy foundation.

Chapter 4

Big Rock #1:

H – Holy Foundation

Healthy foundations are built
on a holy foundation

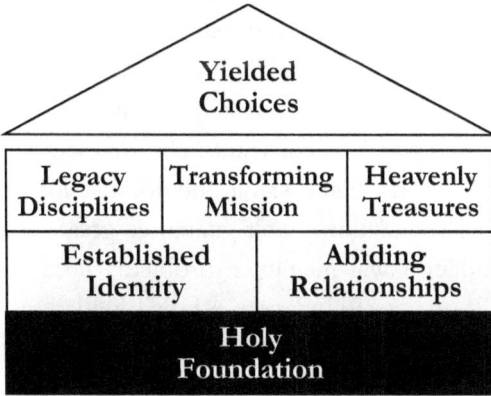

Yielded Choices		
Legacy Disciplines	Transforming Mission	Heavenly Treasures
Established Identity		Abiding Relationships
Holy Foundation		

Build the right *foundation*

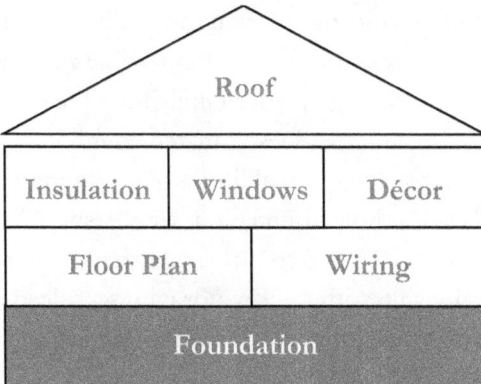

Roof		
Insulation	Windows	Décor
Floor Plan		Wiring
Foundation		

If you want a successful house, build the right foundation. But what's the *right* foundation? It must be strong and stable. It won't shift when conditions shift. It doesn't settle, crack, or collapse, even when stressed. When a foundation is compromised, the house will eventually crumble. You may not yet appreciate the importance of a house's foundation, but you will when things start falling apart.

There's a reason the Tower of Pisa leans – its foundation is only 9 feet deep, and it's built on unstable soil. The Pisa tower is gorgeous with intricately carved marble, but its poor foundation threatens the whole structure. Its builders didn't want the wrong foundation; they just didn't choose the right foundation.

So too, your family needs you to choose the right foundation – a holy foundation – that is stable and doesn't slowly "lean." The right spiritual foundation won't guarantee great results, but the wrong foundation will guarantee problems because everything rises and falls on your foundation. A holy foundation doesn't limit your life; it keeps you from shifting and crumbling.

A great home starts with a great foundation, right? Wrong. A great foundation is crucial, but it serves no purpose if it doesn't fit what's built on it. You need to first choose the kind of life and family you want and then build a foundation to support it.

If you want a happy home, you can build a foundation based on happiness. Granted, that choice has terrible consequences, but at least you're not setting up your family for a life of hypocrisy by building a foundation that doesn't match your life.

Instead, choose the spiritual fitness goal of a spiritually healthy home and build a holy foundation with Jesus Christ as your cornerstone (Eph. 2:20, Acts 4:11). Anchor your family on a personal relationship with the Creator who sacrificed Himself for you and wants a relationship with you. That's the first "H" big rock of a HEALTHY home – H*oly foundation*.

The question isn't "What's the right foundation?" because "no one can lay any foundation other than the one already laid, which is Jesus Christ" (1 Cor. 3:11). The better question is: "Is Jesus *your* foundation?" Are you building your life and family upon Him with things that last?

"If anyone builds on this foundation using gold, silver, costly stones, wood, hay or straw, their work will be shown for what it is, because the Day will bring it to light. It will be revealed with fire, and the fire will test the quality of each person's work" (1 Cor. 3:12-13).

As a Christian, my fear isn't death because that's when I meet Jesus. My fear is having nothing to lay at Jesus' feet (if my works burn up when tested by fire). Therefore, I'm compelled to give Him the very best fire-proof gifts possible. And, surely, one of God's favorite gifts to receive is a home built on a holy foundation of biblical truths and spiritually healthy habits.

Biblical truths don't settle. They don't crack, crumble, or compromise. Here are four truths about who God is and what He does for you. And when you build habits based on these truths, they'll transform your life.

Trinity	*God chose you to be wholly holy*
Light-giver	*God enlightens you to know Him*
Savior	*God offers you eternal life as a free gift*
Creator	*God created you to be His masterpiece*

For each of the 7 Big Rocks, we'll review four habits/truths, along with applications and a practical exercise. And while there are many habits of spiritual health, those unpacked in each chapter will clarify what many of us need – clarity on what vibrant spiritual health looks like and help to take next steps.

The first healthy habit of a holy foundation is to live out the truth that the Trinity God chose you to be wholly holy.

#1 Trinity

God chose you to be wholly holy

He chose us in Him before the creation of the world to be holy and blameless in His sight. – Eph. 1:4

If you want a healthy home, family members need to know that they matter. Not because of what they do, but because they're yours. You love them, and your family isn't whole without them. You'll do anything for them no matter how they respond because they're family. And nowhere is this truer than in God's family.

You matter to God's family. Not because of what you do, but because you're His. You're a perfect fit for what His family needs, and He will love you no matter how you respond.

God's family isn't complete without you. He chose you, created you, and conforms you into His Son's likeness (Rom. 8:29) to spend eternity with Him (Eccl. 3:11, John 3:14-16).

When you wander off, God doesn't leave you. He leaves the ninety-nine to bring you back (Matt. 18:12-14). When you run off, He doesn't run away. He runs to celebrate with you (Luke 15:20). Why? Because His goal is for you to be wholly holy (Eph 1:4).

While this speaks to your value; it says even more about God and how He sets you apart to be positionally holy (Heb. 10:10). At the moment you trust Jesus as your Savior, He declares you holy (1 Pet. 1:16, 2:9). You don't earn it. He places holiness in you so that you can act like who you are – God's holy child.

But to know what God does for you, you need to know God. While God is the all-knowing, all-present, all-powerful creator of the universe, He's also the all-personal God who wants intimacy with you. When God created man, He said, "Let Us make mankind in Our image, in Our likeness" (Gen. 1:26). "Us" and "Our" in that verse is the Trinity – one God with three persons:

God the Father, God the Son, and God the Spirit. All three persons of the Holy Trinity matter. And here's how all three miraculously chose you to be wholly holy.

Three Miracles of Being Chosen by God:

1. **God the Father predestined you**
   "We were also chosen, having been predestined according to the plan of Him who works out everything in conformity with the purpose of His will." – Eph. 1:11

Before you existed, God the Father chose you to be His fearfully, wonderfully made child (Ps. 139:13-14). It was His plan, and His plan always works out (Eph. 1:11). We don't know exactly how He predestines us to become conformed to Jesus' image, but He can and He does. We're called, justified, and glorified for eternity (Rom. 8:29-30). He chose us to know Him (Eph. 1:4). God's character is love (1 John 4:8), so He doesn't want to punish us. But He is also holy, so He must punish our sins (Ex. 34:7). He solved this dilemma in the person of Jesus Christ – God the Son.

2. **God the Son saved you**
   "In order that we, who were the first to put our hope in Christ, might be for the praise of His glory. And you also were included in Christ when you heard the message of truth, the gospel of your salvation." – Eph. 1:12-13a

We were all lost in sin (Rom. 5:8, Eph. 1:7). But the offense of sin was paid by the sufficiency of Jesus Christ. As He hung on the cross, Jesus cried out, "Tetelestai," an accounting term meaning paid in full (John 19:30). He stamps "paid in full" in the record book of your life if you'll confess your sins (1 John 1:9) and repent (Acts 3:19, Luke 13:3). By believing in (i.e., trusting in/relying on) Him, God the Son will forgive you (Col. 3:13, Matt. 9:5-6), save you (Acts 4:12), and remove your sins as far as the east is from the west (Ps. 103:12) so that God the Spirit can seal you.

3. <u>God the Spirit sealed you</u>

"When you believed, you were marked in Him with a seal, the promised Holy Spirit, who is a deposit guaranteeing our inheritance until the redemption of those who are God's possession." – Eph. 1:13b-14

Like an identifying mark on contracts, God the Spirit seals you for eternity. His seal is like a ring pressed into wax to prove you're authentically His. That seal can't be broken, and no one can snatch you from His hand (John 10:28). Nothing can separate you from His love (Rom. 8:38-39), which He offers freely to you. But it requires a personal response from you.

That's the first healthy habit of a holy foundation – being wholly holy because just as God the Trinity who "called you is holy, so be holy in all you do" (1 Pet. 1:15).

The second healthy habit of a holy foundation in Ephesians is allowing God the Light-giver to enlighten you because He desperately wants you to know Him.

#2 Light-giver

God enlightens you to know Him

I pray that the eyes of your heart may be enlightened in order that you may know the hope to which he has called you, the riches of his glorious inheritance in his holy people, and his incomparably great power for us who believe. – Eph. 1:18-19a

Why does God go to such lengths to predestine you, save you, and seal you? Because He desperately wants you to know "the power of his resurrection and participation in his sufferings" (Phil. 3:10). God isn't a distant deity that hopes you'll somehow figure out who He is. He doesn't leave you to wander aimlessly in the dark. He wants you to know Him and make Him known (John 17:3, 26).

God the Light-giver enlightens you to know the truth. Not a truth. Not your truth. THE truth. His Word teaches, reproves, corrects, and trains you for every good work (2 Tim. 3:16-17). He gives you spiritual understanding (Job 32:8, 1 Cor. 2:10) and guides your heart and mind (Phil. 4:7).

He also enlightens you through prayer. He doesn't just shine light on you; His light also shines from within you. According to Ephesians 1:18-19a, He enlightens the eyes of your heart to know His attributes in three ways: His boundless hope, rich inheritance, and incomparable power.

First, God enlightens you to know His boundless hope. That's not a wish; it's a promise. It brings you joy (Rom. 12:12) and it brings Him delight (Ps. 147:11). God's hope is His plan for you (Jer. 29:11) and the reason Scripture exists (Rom. 15:4).

Second, God enlightens you to know His rich inheritance. As His child, your future is secure and glorious (Eph. 1:18). You're rich because He owns it all, and you'll inherit what matters to Him – a place with Him in heaven (John 14:2-4).

And third, God enlightens you to know His incomparable power. Everyone wants power, but no one has the power to be in control because God alone is in control. Through Him, you can do all things because He strengthens you (Phil. 4:13).

Knowing about God, though, isn't the same as knowing Him. How well do you know Him? Here are five essentials of truly knowing Him.

Five Essentials of Truly Knowing God:

1. Love Him

If we truly know God, we'll love Him. Why? Because we'll know that God is love and that He goes to extraordinary lengths to spend eternity with us. For example, the more I know my wife, the more I love her, but her love can't compare to God's love.

God loves us so much, He sent His only Son to die for us (John 3:16), even if we reject Him.

2. Believe in Him

If we truly love God, we'll believe in Him. Why? Because His love draws us to believe. We can't fully grasp the simplicity and depth of a love that only requires us to become like a child (Luke 18:17) and believe Him with a mustard seed of faith (Matt. 17:20).

3. Trust Him

If we truly believe in God, we'll trust Him. Why? Because we'll know His character, and His character is true. He's trustworthy and fair. He's caring, approachable, compassionate, forgiving, and so much more. But we must allow the God of eternity to become our God for eternity.

4. Obey Him

If we truly trust God, we'll obey Him. Why? Because we gladly obey who we truly trust. That kind of obedience isn't reluctant or resentful. It's joyful even if it's painful at the time. Don't be like Solomon, who had to try it all before realizing it all comes down to: "fear God and keep his commandments" (Eccl. 12:13).

5. Experience Him

If we truly obey God, we'll experience Him. Why? Because God's salvation lets us experience eternal life in heaven as well as abundant life on earth (John 10:10). Abundant life experiences abundant hope (Rom. 15:13), and once we've experienced Him, nothing else satisfies.

You can't fully know God, but He fully knows you. He clearly sees you. He unconditionally loves you. And He desperately wants you to know Him, which is possible only because of the next truth and healthy habit of a holy foundation – God the Savior offers you eternal life as a free gift.

#3 Savior

God offers you eternal life as a free gift

For it is by grace you have been saved, through faith—and this is not from yourselves, it is the gift of God—not by works, so that no one can boast. – Eph. 2:8-9

As a young man, I was compelled to understand other religions in hopes of better embracing my own. Much to my surprise, my conclusion was that all religions, except Christianity, do two things: (1) they try to earn their own salvation and (2) they say Jesus Christ is less than God the Son at birth.

All other religions must do this because everything in life rests on two pillars of Christianity: (1) we can't earn our salvation and (2) Jesus was, is, and always will be the eternal Son of God.

First, it's logical to think that God expects us to earn our way into heaven – that our good must outweigh our bad. But that's not God's plan. His plan is crystal clear and infinitely superior: we're saved by God's grace through faith in Him (Eph. 2:8-9). Faith doesn't save us. God's grace saves us. Faith is just the means by which we access His grace.

As shown in the next healthy habit, the Creator God created us to do good works. But good works don't get us into heaven; they just determine the rewards for people who get into heaven. Good works don't cause faith; they flow from faith. We tend to get it backward because we want to be proud of what we do. Therefore, we need clarity on what salvation is and is not:

- Salvation is receiving God's grace, not earning God's grace.

- Salvation births good works, not boasting about good works.

Second, all other religions try to diminish Jesus because if He alone is the way, the truth, and the life (John 14:6), then all other ways lead to hell. And by making Jesus to be just a person who became like God, they too hope to become God-like.

Jesus, though, wasn't just a man. He is the Son of God who became a man – fully God and fully man. He lived a perfect life, died on a cross, and rose from the dead to pay for our sins, which He offers us as a free gift. We can't achieve it; we just receive it. But we must receive it with eternal urgency.

In a remote village of Kenya, I saw hundreds of people accept Jesus as Savior, although they had never heard of Him. And in Dallas, I watched a young Mexican mom become a child of God, despite speaking little English and having two infants crying at her feet. And the person who shared the gospel with her was nervous and unorganized. Nevertheless, she became a Christian because the gospel saves, not us. We just share it.

Once, as I shared the gospel with a man on the night of a Super Tuesday presidential primary, his estranged wife called him out of the blue to tell him to listen to the people in his apartment. Wow. And after praying to receive Jesus as his Savior, he proclaimed, "It really IS Super Tuesday!"

No matter how we try to complicate salvation and add things to it, it's still a free gift from a loving God. And while salvation isn't just intellectually agreeing to who Jesus is, it's also not one of these three transactions to try to get God to love us:

Three Transactions That are Not Salvation:

1. A swap

God doesn't swap favors. You don't scratch God's back so that He will scratch yours. After surrendering your life to Him, He expects you to live for Him, but you don't have to get cleaned up before you come to Him. He cleans you up. He does all the work; you just accept it and live according to it.

2. A demand

No matter how much God loves you, He doesn't demand that you accept Him. He lets you choose. Like a true gentleman, He knocks on your heart and invites you to let Him in (Rev. 3:20). But He goes only where He's invited.

3. A negotiation

You don't negotiate with God. Salvation is on His terms. You can't pick and choose the parts you like because He paid the price for your sins. God's salvation works for all and is the same for all because it covers all and satisfies all.

When I worked at CiCi's Pizza, we had limited time only (LTO) pizzas. But at some point, our LTO's went away because they were limited. God's salvation, though, isn't an LTO. It's limitless. It never goes away. It's the offer of offers from the King of kings and the Lord of lords. But you don't know how much limited time you have to accept His offer. Thus, you need to create a healthy habit of the fourth truth of a holy foundation: God the Creator created you to be His masterpiece.

#4 Creator

God created you to be His masterpiece

For we are God's handiwork, created in Christ Jesus to do good works, which God prepared in advance for us to do. – Eph. 2:10

Ephesians 2:8-9 says God offers us salvation as a free gift. And the next verse says why – to be His handiwork, His masterpiece. We're set free, set apart, and set up to do Master-worthy works. We're not saved by good works; we do good works because we are saved. And through God's salvation, we find the reason He created us – to share the life transformation found in Him. God creates everything (especially you) for His purpose.

I'll never forget training a group of seminary students on interviewing and seeing their shock when I said, "You're the answer to someone's prayer." They knew that God uses people to do miraculous things, but they'd never considered that they could be the miracle that others pray for. When you believe that, it changes everything. You act, think, and prepare differently because you're God's masterpiece, His apostle ("sent one") to do Master-worthy works for Him. Here are two examples that still give me goosebumps of how God uses even me.

When I started a new Controller job, they called me, "Holy Roller Controller." But a co-worker, Scott, wasn't a fan. He told me, "Two things I don't talk about: religion and politics!" Well, a year later after becoming friends, I invited Scott to lunch to share the gospel. And, sure enough, Scott received Jesus as his Savior. As we left the restaurant, with tears in his eyes, Scott said, "The day you came to work here, I went home and told my wife: 'God brought Tim Alba here for me!'"

Another company I joined had many Christians, but you never know who, like Jeff, is just acting saved. Years later, when Jeff and I met to discuss spiritual matters, he did something I had never seen. He took notes. He wrote my gospel outline on a napkin as I shared it. Clearly, God had Scott and Jeff ready. I was just a conduit. And so are you. You're created by a masterful God to be a chosen, enlightened, saved masterpiece for His glory. Here are four ways that He is masterful.

Four Ways That God is Masterful:

1. God is Master-sized

God chooses even the least of us for His God-sized plans. But like the Exodus Jews who were afraid to enter the Promised Land because giants lived there, we let obstacles frighten us. Please don't focus on the giants. Focus on God's Master-sized mission for you and His unlimited provision to make it happen.

2. God is Master-minded

God is the great Mastermind. We may think we play chess while others play checkers. But as the ultimate chess master, God sees the big picture because He is the big picture. He sees beyond our next move. He knows the end and how to get there. Thus, we must trust Him even when nothing makes sense.

3. God is Master-worthy

God has a Master-worthy purpose for you. You might doubt that or doubt your worth sometimes. But no matter what you may think, you are Master-worthy because God says you're worthy. And that settles it.

4. God is Master-full

God does nothing halfway. He's fully right and fully sufficient. And He wants you to be all-in or all-out, not lukewarm (Rev. 3:15-16). Everyone He calls is fully blessed. It may not be exactly what you want, but it's exactly what you need when you need it. And, no, that's not a cliché. I know it's true because the Bible says it's true (Phil 4:19) and I've seen it happen over and over again.

Now, let's take a moment to consider the holiness of *your* foundation. Using a scale of 1-to-10 (low-to-high), please score how well your life reflects the below four healthy habits/truths and write those four scores in the "You" column, along with the total score and average score.

Holy Foundation		**You**	**Home**
<u>Trinity:</u>	*God chose you to be wholly holy*	___	___
<u>Light-giver:</u>	*God enlightens you to know Him*	___	___
<u>Savior:</u>	*God offers you eternal life as a free gift*	___	___
<u>Creator:</u>	*God created you to be His masterpiece*	___	___
	Total	___	___
	/4 = Average	☐	☐

Next, in the "Home" column above, do the same for your family. As noted earlier, although each family member is unique, write an overall score for how well your family reflects each of these four statements, as well as your home's total and average scores. Later, we'll summarize the average scores to take next steps in your spiritual journey.

Which of the above four healthy habits/truths is the lowest for you? Which is lowest for your home? And which is the highest for you and your home? The lowest score is likely an area of needed growth and a place to start, while the highest score may be where you can impact others by leveraging a strength.

Next, please pick one of the four healthy habits/truths that you'll commit to improve. Growing all of them would be great but start with one. That is, do you want you and your family to grow most by living the truth that God is the Trinity, Light-giver, Savior, or Creator? (Please write your answer below.)

The Holy foundation habit I'll grow is: _____

Spiritual growth is essential, but do you ever struggle with feeling like you don't do enough for God? While it's true that faith without works is dead (James 2:14-17), you don't have to measure up to a self-imposed standard. Just live and share the gospel that God offers. But to share the gospel, you have to know the gospel. Here's a simple, powerful way to share the gospel – God's good news – with anyone in need of a Savior.

Exercise: "G-O-S-P-E-L"

Easily share God's good news

A few days before graduation, a group of us were talking about life after high school. Most of us would go to college or work on a family farm. Then Lynette, whom I hardly knew despite growing up with her since kindergarten, said, "What are you gonna do, Tim? I always thought you'd be a preacher or something."

Wow! All those years, Lynette had been watching to see if my faith was real. She may have been a Christian, but I didn't know since I hadn't asked. It was the first time I realized that people are more willing to listen to the gospel than I'm willing to share it.

For years, I hid behind excuses like: "They won't listen," "I've messed up," or "I don't know what to say." Well, turns out, Lynette was listening, open, and not expecting me to be perfect. I just needed to be ready. So, I've taken various evangelism classes, the best of which is an acrostic of G-O-S-P-E-L, created by John Meador. It's so clear and easy that its six core points were already included in this chapter – all taken from Ephesians 2.

G – God's character: "Because of his great love for us, God, who is rich in mercy" (Eph. 2:4).

God's character is fully loving and fully holy. He is rich in mercy and love, but since He is also holy, He must punish sin.

O – Offense of sin: "Even when we were dead in transgressions" (Eph. 2:5).

All of us sin and fall short of God's glory (Rom. 3:23). God is offended by our sin, which separates us from Him until Jesus Christ did something miraculous to change that.

S – Sufficiency of Christ: "Made us alive with Christ" (Eph. 2:5).

We can know God because of the life, death, and resurrection of His Son, Jesus Christ, whose free gift of eternal life is sufficient to save us. There's nothing we can do to earn it. We simply receive it and trust the sufficiency of His sacrifice for our sins.

P – Personal response: "For it is by grace you have been saved, through faith" (Eph. 2:8).

The only way to become a child of God is through a personal response to follow Jesus Christ. We're not saved by our good works, our family, or our church. We're saved only by believing in Jesus and accepting His free gift of eternal life.

E – Eternal urgency: "In order that in the coming ages he might show the incomparable riches of his grace" (Eph. 2:7).

Our options are to either choose heaven through faith in Christ or spend eternity in hell. Therefore, we need an urgency to know Him and tell others about Him.

L – Life transformation: "We are God's handiwork, created in Christ Jesus to do good works" (Eph. 2:10).

Salvation isn't just a ticket out of hell; it's also a ticket to transformation. We're made new from the inside out. And we're drawn to do Master-worthy works for our Master.

There's nothing more important than becoming a child of God. And once you're His child, the best thing you can do is share and live the gospel – the good news of God's salvation for mankind.

Sharing the gospel isn't just for ministers; it's what we're all called to do. And now, if you can spell GOSPEL, you can share it! If you'd like to see it too, watch John Meador share it at www.johnmeador.com. With a little practice, you'll "be prepared to give an answer to everyone who asks you to give the reason for the hope that you have" (1 Pet. 3:15).

Once you have a foundation of who God is, you're ready to embrace who God says you are – the second big rock of a HEALTHY home: E – Established identity.

Chapter 5

Big Rock #2:

E – Established Identity

Healthy self-identity is
God's established identity for you

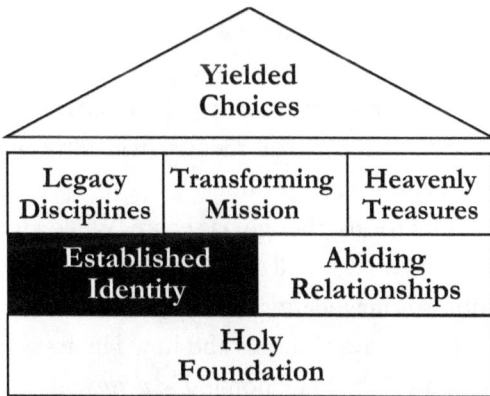

```
                    /\
                   /  \
                  / Yielded \
                 /  Choices  \
                /_____\
                |Legacy |Transforming|Heavenly |
                |Disciplines| Mission |Treasures|
                |_____|_____|_____|
                |Established   | Abiding        |
                | Identity     | Relationships  |
                |_____|_____|
                |        Holy                   |
                |      Foundation               |
                |_____|
```

Frame your house
by following the *floor plan*

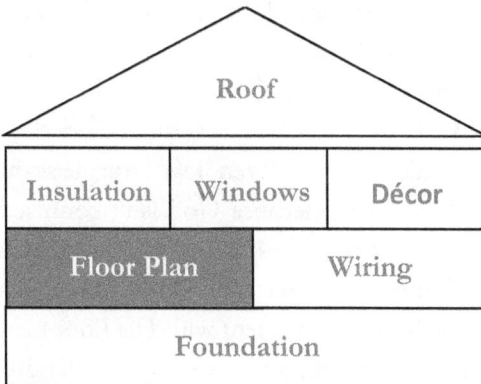

```
                    /\
                   /  \
                  /Roof\
                 /_____\
                |Insulation|Windows| Décor |
                |_____|_____|_____|
                |Floor Plan   | Wiring       |
                |_____|_____|
                |       Foundation           |
                |_____|
```

A strong foundation is crucial, but you don't pick a house to build based on the foundation. You pick it based on a floor plan that establishes the relationships and features of rooms designed for your benefit. So, after building the right foundation for your floor plan, you need to frame it according to that floor plan.

Once you pick a floor plan, though, you must follow it because you've already built a foundation to support it. The same applies to your family. You need to pick a spiritual floor plan – a spiritual identity – that aligns with a Holy foundation and follow it. Why? Because your spiritual floor plan will define your identity.

A solid self-identity is key to understanding your core values. But if you try to separate your personal identity from your spiritual identity, your personal identity will flip-flop based on circumstances, culture, and emotions.

God's identity for us, though, is secure. While He gives each of us a unique mission (as we'll see later), He also created all of us with a common spiritual identity based on what He wants for all of us. It's what God says about us and how He designed us – the "E" big rock of a HEALTHY home: *Established identity*.

As Jesus followers, our job is to frame our life by following His floor plan for us. Instead of asking: "Who am I?", ask: "Who does God say I am?" Because when you follow what God says about you, you'll experience all the relationships and features that He designed for your benefit.

We may not always like God's design for us, but it's our spiritual DNA. It never changes. It's established. So, we need to understand it and embrace it. Even if we struggle sometimes with our identity, don't worry because God isn't confused. Once we become His child, we're always His child. And, thankfully, when our personal identity slides away from His established identity for us, He brings us back in alignment with His floor plan.

Problems arise, though, when we confuse identity with roles. I'm a husband, dad, and grandpa, but that's not my identity. A

DNA test said I'm 88% South European, but that's not my character. I'm a business executive, but that's not who I am. No matter what I think of myself, I am who God says I am.

A healthy self-identity is God's established identity for you. God made you in His image for His purpose. God's the designer; you're the builder. If you try to be your own designer or if you refuse to work with your Designer, you'll mess it up. But instead of being booted from His family, God hugs you even tighter because you're family. He loves you anyway; while still expecting you to follow the floor plan He established for you.

God has room in His family for all kinds of people with all kinds of problems. We don't need to have it all together, but together we have it all!. We just need to align our personal identity with our established identity – who God says we are and who He created us to be.

God says you are His adopted child that He uniquely gifted to be a steward of His grace and a temple in which His Spirit dwells. If you'll grow in these truths and turn them into habits, your family will never be the same. I know because if they could transform my family and me, God can do the same for you.

Adopted	*You're adopted into God's family*
Gifted	*You're gifted to equip God's church*
Steward	*You're a steward of God's grace*
Temple	*You're God's holy dwelling place*

God's established identity for you is universal, yet personal. It instills confidence, belonging, and well-being. It forges value and instills values. Like spiritual guardrails, it keeps you out of the ditch while allowing you to drive in your own lane. Your established identity doesn't restrict you; it empowers you to be all that God created you to be as His adopted child.

#1 Adopted

You're adopted into God's family

He predestined us for adoption to sonship through Jesus Christ, in accordance with his pleasure and will. — Eph. 1:5

I get choked up every time my friend talks about her adopted grandson, Kai. She loves each grandchild, of course, but this little guy has a special place in her heart. Kai's adoption was a long, heart-wrenching process, but it was settled once and for all when the judge slammed his gavel and said that from that moment on, Kai would forever be a member of my friend's family.

Most of us are blessed with a biological family, but no one appreciates family more than adoptees of loving homes. They didn't earn a new identity, but they got one when they were blessed with adoption. We all want these blessings, but only spiritually healthy homes can fully enjoy them because they revel in being adopted into God's family.

To understand God's adoption, though, you need to understand the biblical context of Roman adoption. Roman adoptees could not be disowned. Biological kids could be disowned, but not adoptees. Adoptees received a new identity and a full, immediate inheritance as legal heirs for life. They didn't wait for an adopting parent's death to share in family possessions because their inheritance began at the moment of adoption. Prior debts were erased and replaced with new rights.

So too, "the Spirit you received brought about your adoption to sonship. And by him we cry, 'Abba Father'" (Rom. 8:15). Abba – a term of intimacy, reverence, and obedience – reflects a permanent, intimate love. God reaches out of heaven to identify personally with lost people like you and me to bring us home as His child (Eph. 1:5). But until you experience the three blessings of God's adoption, you can't truly appreciate them.

Three Blessings of God's Adoption:

1. Unconditional love

Love often comes with conditions: "I'll love you if you __."
We've all experienced conditional love, but God's "agape" love is
different. Agape love is unconditional, selfless, pure, and
sacrificial – a supernatural gift from a supernatural God.

Like entitled kids, though, we often act entitled to God's love.
Still, He gives us unconditional agape love, and He expects us to
pass it along to other spiritual adoptees who need it too.

2. Undeserved acceptance

Ever wonder why God protects orphans so much? (Ps. 68:5, Ps.
10:14, James 1:27) It represents His care for us – spiritual orphans
in great need and unable to return the favor. It's also a picture of
how we long for the Father's undeserved acceptance.

So too, we were all lost and hopeless until God adopted us
into His family. We can't demand His adoption. We just receive
it and treasure it because it's who we are now and forever will be.
So, don't get mad when lost people act lost, because we too were
spiritual orphans before God adopted us.

3. Unwavering stability

God's adoption births unwavering stability. Like a no-returns
policy, God won't return us like an unwanted purchase – proof
of the height, breath, and depth of His love (Eph. 3:18).

Jesus can identify and empathize with us because He was
tested like us, yet without sin (Heb. 4:15). He took on our identity
so that we can take on His identity as co-heirs awaiting bodily
redemption (Rom. 8:17, 23). No longer slaves to sin, we're free to
be adopted heirs (Gal. 4:3-7) of His unconditional love,
undeserved acceptance, and unwavering stability. And we don't
need a gavel to finalize the fact that we're His and that, as we'll
see next, He has gifted each of us to equip His church.

#2 Gifted

You're gifted to equip God's church

*To each one of us grace has been given as Christ apportioned it –
Eph. 4:7*

*Christ himself gave the apostles, the prophets, the evangelists, the
pastors and teachers, to equip his people for works of service, so that
the body of Christ may be built up until we all reach unity in the
faith and in the knowledge of the Son of God and become
mature, attaining to the whole measure of the fullness of Christ. –
Eph. 4:11-13*

Although I dreamed of being a pro athlete, it became obvious
early on that I was destined for a career in business, not sports. I
had the desire to be a great athlete, but not the physical gift.

I also wanted spiritual gifts that I admired in others. Like me,
have you ever said, "If only I was __, God could really use me"?
If so, no matter how you fill in that blank, you're wrong. God's
gifts are perfect to accomplish His purpose (Eph. 4:7-13). If He
gave you the spiritual gift of evangelism, evangelize faithfully
(Eph 4:11). If it's teaching, teach as unto God. If serving, serve
well. You don't choose your spiritual gifts; you just choose if
you'll use them for His glory.

It's the same with vocational and family gifts. If you're a nurse
or electrician, be faithful. If you're a parent or sibling, be faithful.
No matter your talents or roles, God equips you to equip His
church for unity and maturity (Eph. 4:12-13).

God's gifts for you align perfectly with His plans for you. His
gifts are like instruments to be played in harmony with others. But
if we don't play what He orchestrates, we'll be a noisy mess. In
fact, we're told in 1 Corinthians 14 to pursue the gifts God gives
us, not the gifts we prefer. In Jesus' parable of the talents, "A man
. . . called his servants and entrusted his wealth to them. To one

he gave five bags of gold, to another two bags, and to another one bag, each according to his ability" (Matt. 25:14-15a).

Have you ever asked God to be the one with five bags, not just one? I have. If so, you might mean well too, but be careful. Before you ask God for more, be faithful with what you have.

Your gifts don't determine your identity; they reflect your identity as God's child. God apportions your gifts according to your ability (Eph. 4,7, Matt. 25:15). He will hold you accountable to maximize them (Matt 25:19) and equip the church (Eph. 4:12). What gifts has God given you (Eph. 4:7)?

Instead of being jealous of other people's gifts, be zealous with yours. For example, my son wanted his music engineering internship to be more like his friends' experiences. Nevertheless, Josh served zealously and eventually helped mix an album for Kirk Whalum that debuted #1 on Billboard's Contemporary Jazz Chart. When I met Mr. Whalum years later, he raved about Josh's music skills, but he also praised Josh's Christian character. And while I was proud of my son, I was reminded that Josh simply did what we're all required to do – leverage our gifts to equip the church. Here are four questions to help you do the same.

Four Questions to Leverage Your Gifts:

1. What's your motivation?

Who do you build up? Others or yourself? I can't know your motives, but I can see who you're edifying. And while God wants you to leverage your gifts, what He wants even more is a motivation of faithfulness.

2. What's your pride?

Does your pride ever get in the way? Of course, it does. Pride can be cocky and unteachable, or it can be subtle and self-righteous. But pride is always selfish and sinful. Selfish, though, isn't the same as self-interest. It's in your self-interest to build up your family and the church. So, are your actions in your self-interest or just selfish?

3. Who's your audience?

Who are you trying to please? You? Your family? Others? You can't meet someone else's needs if your main audience is you. Meeting other people's needs starts with knowing their needs, which starts with humbly asking, intentionally listening, and continually learning what they need.

4. What's your effectiveness?

How effective are you? Do you make people better, or do you mistake effort for effectiveness? God doesn't demand results, but He doesn't delight in mediocrity. If you're ineffective, pray for wisdom, revelation, and discernment to improve. And while you're at it, revisit your motivation, pride, and audience.

Have you ever given a gift to a child that just plays with the box? Don't be that child. Make your Heavenly Father proud of your next healthy habit – being a faithful steward of the gifts He gives you.

#3 Steward

You're a steward of God's grace

You have heard about the administration of God's grace that was given to me for you. – Eph. 3:2

Many people complain about owners while wanting to be one. Why? Because they want the benefits of ownership without the burdens. I've been both – an owner and an employee. But your role in a company (or a family) doesn't alter your responsibility or your opportunity to be something far more rewarding than ownership – stewardship.

A steward is also different from an employee. Employees prove themselves to get more, but stewards improve themselves to give more. Employees get a paycheck; stewards get an opportunity to serve. We don't have to be a steward. We *get* to be a steward. And what is required of a steward is to be found faithful (1 Cor. 4:2). "Each of you should use whatever gift you have received to serve others, as faithful stewards of God's grace" (1 Pet. 4:10). Jesus agreed in Matthew 25:15b-21, as the parable of the talents continues:

> Then he went on his journey. The man who had received five bags of gold went at once and put his money to work and gained five bags more. So also, the one with two bags of gold gained two more. But the man who had received one bag went off, dug a hole in the ground and hid his master's money. After a long time the master of those servants returned and settled accounts with them. The man who had received five bags of gold brought the other five. 'Master,' he said, 'you entrusted me with five bags of gold. See, I have gained five more.' His master replied, 'Well done, good and faithful servant! You have been faithful with a few things; I will put you in charge of many things. Come and share your master's happiness!'"

Jesus then proceeds with the second servant:

> "The man with two bags of gold also came. 'Master,' he said, 'you entrusted me with two bags of gold; see, I have gained two more.' His master replied, 'Well done, good and faithful servant! You have been faithful with a few things; I will put you in charge of many things. Come and share your master's happiness!'" (Matt. 25:22-23)

The master expected similar faithfulness, not similar profits. So too, God judges you based on what you do with what He gives you, not what He gives someone else. Both servants received a financial reward, but their greatest reward was entering into the master's presence. Then, sadly, there's the third servant:

"Then the man who had received one bag of gold came. 'Master,' he said, 'I knew that you are a hard man, harvesting where you have not sown and gathering where you have not scattered seed. So I was afraid and went out and hid your gold in the ground. See, here is what belongs to you.' His master replied, 'You wicked, lazy servant!'" (Matt. 25:24-26).

This lazy servant didn't blow his money; he blew his opportunity. He was judged harshly because he acted like an employee, not a steward. He tried excuses and spin, instead of apologies and repentance. Regardless of his intentions, he wasn't faithful, and that's never acceptable. Here are four more ways in Matthew 25 that God rewards stewards, not employees.

Four Rewards of Faithful Stewardship:

1. More affirmation
There's nothing like affirmation, and there's no affirmation like God's "Well done!" While faithfulness, not praise, must be our goal, imagine the thrill of hearing "Well done!" as Jesus wraps His arms around you, holds you tight, and affirms your stewardship.

2. More work
The reward for faithfulness isn't rest; it's more work. Stewards are motivated by being entrusted with more opportunities to please the owner. If you don't want more work, don't be faithful. But the joy of faithfulness is priceless, and the alternative is tragic.

3. More joy
More faithfulness causes more joy because you get to be with the Master. If the Prodigal Son's brother had this joy, he would have celebrated his brother's return, not gotten angry that his loving father forgave his wayward brother (Luke 15:28-32).

4. More abundance
The first servant started with the most, earned the most, and even got the unfaithful servant's portion. If that seems unfair, you're

not thinking like God whose goal is abundance – growing His kingdom (1 Tim. 2:4) and the faithful stewards who maximize it.

Stewardship is often seen only in the context of money. But while stewardship includes money, it's much more. Instead of first giving themselves to God (2 Cor. 8:5), some people write checks. Others serve but withhold their money. Both approaches miss the mark because they miss your identity as a steward.

Don't rob God of your money. Don't rob people of your ability to bless them. And don't rob yourself of the Master's joy that flows from being who God says you are – His holy temple.

#4 Temple

You're God's holy dwelling place

In him the whole building is joined together and rises to become a holy temple in the Lord. And in him you too are being built together to become a dwelling in which God lives by his Spirit. – Eph. 2:21-22

More than ever, an insidious danger attacks our hearts and finances – financial identity theft. Over one million Americans annually are victims of those who steal our identity, kill our confidence, and destroy our credit.

Families also face a danger that attacks our hearts and minds – spiritual identity theft. If not properly protected, we'll fall victim to a spiritual enemy who seeks to steal, kill, and destroy (John 10:10). Both types of identity theft are painful, but spiritual identity theft is fully preventable.

Yes, you'll endure spiritual attacks and, yes, you must keep your guard up. But your spiritual enemy is powerless unless you let him steal your identity. He can hack your life, but he can't steal your joy unless you let him (John 16:22). He can destroy your sense of security, but he can't destroy your eternal security (John

10:27-29). As God's child, you're God's temple, His holy dwelling place. God's Spirit takes up residence and lives in you.

Please don't try to be your own temple. Be who God says you are – His temple built on the cornerstone of Jesus Christ (Eph. 2:20). Sure, you'll sometimes crumble or get worn down, but God will still work through you because His Spirit works in you "to fulfill His good purpose" (Phil. 2:13).

Imagine what would happen if you were to live totally aware that God is living in you and working through you. How would it alter your thoughts, words, and actions? How would it affect your relationships? How would it change what you watch when no one is watching you?

I used to tell my young sons: "The real test of a man is what you do in a hotel room by yourself and no one is there to watch." They didn't understand the implications and they acted like they didn't hear me. But years later, I learned that they were listening after all when we created a family mission statement,.

Of the twelve promises we made to God in our family mission statement, one came from my preteen son, Josh, who wanted: "We will passionately pursue you when no one is watching." Wow. Even though he was too young to understand why this promise was so incredibly important, it showed me that he was beginning to want what he needs to be faithful.

Did Josh always look like a godly temple and live up to that promise to God? No. None of us do. But ten years later at Josh's wedding rehearsal dinner, I listened to his groomsmen brag about his godly character. And I thought back to the phrase Josh wanted in our mission statement ten years earlier. I couldn't see his choices at college, but through his groomsmen I saw that Josh was living out his established identity as God's holy temple, which includes these three pillars:

Three Pillars of Being God's Holy Temple:

1. Intentional pursuit of God

Before Ryan became my son-in-law, he asked if he could pursue Leslie. I had never heard of "pursuing" someone, but I admired him for asking. Even better, after a decade of marriage (and three kids), Ryan is still pursuing her.

Spiritual health is much the same. Being God's holy temple starts with intentionally pursuing Him. And it's sustained through a fresh relationship with the God who never stops pursuing us.

2. Intimate relationship with God

Being God's holy temple isn't a casual dating relationship. And it's not a marriage that has lost its spark. It's staying madly in love with Jesus and doing anything to spend the rest of your days in a growing, intimate relationship with Him. And like a great marriage, it takes work. A lot of work.

How do we stay madly in love with God? One way is prayer. My family's favorite is worship music. Another is reading the Bible in fresh ways. For example, I sometimes read through the Bible in a year. One year, I camped out in 1 Corinthians and wrote 300 verse-by-verse devotionals. For decades, I read the Proverb of the day (31 chapters for 31 days). For a couple years, I read the same chapters two days in a row (it's amazing what you see new on the second day). More important than the method, though, is that you stay madly in love with the Messiah.

3. Impactful witness for God

If you'll intentionally pursue and intimately know God, you'll be an impactful witness for Him. You'll find real hope and real life. You'll be joined together with Him and rise to become His holy temple (Eph. 2:21-22). And you'll find freedom. "Where the Spirit of the Lord is, there is freedom" (2 Cor. 3:17).

As we'll do with each of the 7 Big Rocks, please take a moment to consider this chapter's four healthy habits. On a scale of 1 to 10 (low to high), score how well you and your home live out these four truths of Established identity. Then total them and write your averages in the You and Home columns, which we'll use later. Also, please write one healthy habit – Adopted, Gifted, Steward, or Temple – that you want most to grow.

Established Identity		You	Home
<u>Adopted</u>:	*You're adopted into God's family*	___	___
<u>Gifted</u>:	*You're gifted to equip God's church*	___	___
<u>Steward</u>:	*You're a steward of God's grace*	___	___
<u>Temple</u>:	*You're God's holy dwelling place*	___	___
	Total	___	___
	/4 = Average	☐	☐

The Established identity habit I'll grow is: _____

Embracing your identity in Christ requires you to know both your unique qualities and the established identity shared by all of us. In order to better understand how these two mesh, here's an exercise from *Well Done, Mom & Dad!*. You simply share three words to describe each family member's character. It's called "Family Portraits" because you get a "portrait" of the unique features that others see in you.

Exercise: "Family Portraits"

Paint your picture in three words

One of the times we did this exercise, my son added a visual element. He created a page for each person with their photo at the top. Then, he added photos of the other family members and their three words to describe that person. For example, here's Anna's "Family Portrait" – the three words that describe what each of us appreciate most about Anna.

ANNA ALBA

LOVING
GRACE-FILLED
TRUE

SERVANT-HEARTED
COMPASSIONATE
TENDER

WELCOMING
GIVING
LOVING

SELFLESS
THOUGHTFUL
GENUINE

FUN!
CHRISTMAS!
INTERCESSOR

PARTIES!
LOVING
GRACE

LOVING
SELFLESS
GENTLE

This exercise is powerful, in part, because it's simple and personal. If your family is like mine, you'll laugh as well as cry discussing each other's qualities, you'll poke fun at each other, and you'll celebrate each other's unique qualities.

Each time we've done this exercise, I've learned something about my family and me. It encourages and challenges me to be a better spouse, parent, and grandparent. It helps me better understand and serve my family. And it sears lasting memories I wouldn't trade for anything.

Because it had been five years since we did this Family Portraits exercise, I recently sent everyone's three words on a family group text. Amidst a combination of praise and friendly banter, it highlighted how their lives had changed after they had kids and careers. But it also showed how everyone's unique character was still intact.

My favorite memory from this exercise came when Emily had just become my daughter-in-law. At the time, I didn't know much about Emily, other than as a professional ballerina, she seemed to have the world by the tail. On the surface, everything seemed great. But I didn't know she was battling severe depression. I'll never forget her reactions as she read what we saw in her – that she's loved just like she is. She doesn't have to perform or measure up. She's accepted. She's safe with us.

Years later, Emily is thriving on the inside too, a testimony of how God uses all kinds of people and experiences (including this exercise) to bring healing and peace to anyone whose identity is found in Him. Then again, that's what this chapter and exercise do. They help us learn who we are, both individually and collectively in Christ.

And once we're secure in our established identity, we're ready to connect with God and others through the next big rock of a HEALTHY home: A – Abiding relationships.

Chapter 6

Big Rock #3:

A – Abiding Relationships

Healthy relationships flow
from abiding in God

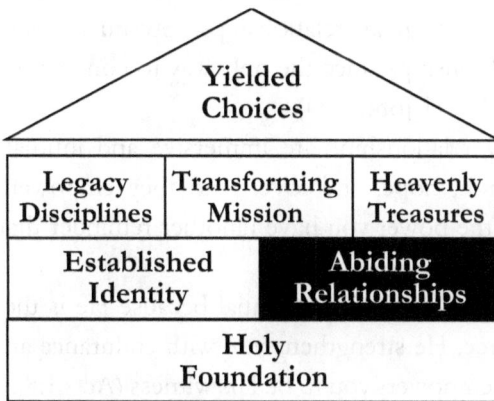

Yielded Choices		
Legacy Disciplines	Transforming Mission	Heavenly Treasures
Established Identity	Abiding Relationships	
Holy Foundation		

Connect your house to the
power source with *wiring*

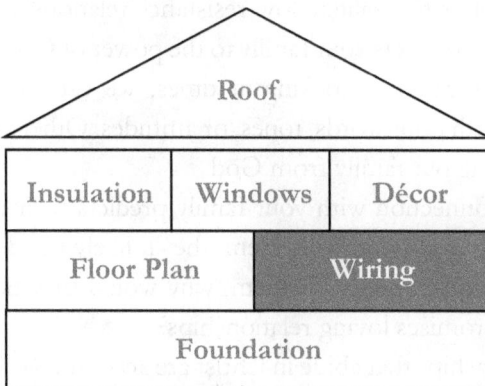

Roof		
Insulation	Windows	Décor
Floor Plan	Wiring	
Foundation		

A house without wiring has no power. So, after building a foundation and framing your house, you need to connect it to the power source with wiring – a low-resistance path for power to flow. If you've ever worked with wiring, though, you know it can be emotionally and physically shocking (pun intended) unless you stick to proven standards. So too, families lack power without spiritual wiring – the "A" big rock of HEALTHY: *Abiding relationships.*

The value of relationships can't be overstated, but we need more than just great relationships. Spiritual health requires abiding relationships since the only way to connect to God is by abiding in Him (1 John 3:24).

Abiding relationships are immersive and intimate. They're wired in faith, hope, and love. And they empower others to experience the power you have (another reminder that a healthy home starts with a healthy you).

Connecting to God is essential because He is the one True Power Source. He strengthens you with endurance and patience (Col. 1:11), empowers you to be His witness (Acts 1:8), and works through you beyond your imagination (Eph. 3:20). Accessing His power enables you to do all things (Phil. 4:13) and receive what you seek according to His will (1 John 5:14-15).

Your job is to facilitate low-resistance relationships and be a conduit that connects your family to the power of God. And since relationships can be shocking at times, we can't lower God's standards with poor words, tones, or attitudes. Otherwise, we risk disconnecting our family from God.

Your connection with your family predicts their connection with God. If you bond with them, they'll likely bond with God. But if you don't bond with them, why would they bond with a God who promises loving relationships?

Relationships that abide in Christ are accountable. They trust. They assume the best, not the worst. They resolve, not fester.

They care, commit, grow, and laugh together. They edify. They reside and endure. They bear good fruit because they're rooted in God's good vine (John 15:4). And, most importantly, they reflect God's agape love – the unconditional, unbreakable, empathetic, sacrificial love modeled by Jesus.

We can abide with God when we have a close proximity to Him, a humble posture before Him, and a secure place with Him. This allows us to know Him, live in Him, and remain true to Him.

An abiding, agape relationship with God is possible because He agape loved us first (1 John 4:19). His Spirit guides us and His Word instructs us how to model agape love that powerfully submits, gives love-respect, forgives, and prays.

Submission	*Submit my wants to your needs*
Love-respect	*Give my love-respect; earn yours*
Forgiveness	*Show compassion by truly forgiving*
Prayer	*Duct tape relationships with prayer*

My favorite example of abiding relationships is my wife. While relationships come more naturally to Anna, she works hard to build them. The secret to her relationships, though, is the source of her relationships – she abides with Jesus Christ. And that's not unique to Anna because all of us can experience abiding relationships by living out Christ's words: "If you keep my commands, you will (abide) in my love, just as I have kept my Father's commands and (abide) in his love" (John 15:10).

Love is a choice, but Anna makes it easy. How about you? Do you make it easy for people to love you and God?

The surprising thing about building abiding relationships, however, is that they don't start with love. Instead, they start with submission.

#1 Submission

Submit my wants to your needs

Submit to one another out of reverence for Christ. – Eph. 5:21

Other than loving my Lord, the best thing I can do for my kids is to love my wife. Everything good in my kids flows from a mom who loves them and feels loved. Since our freshman year in college, Anna and I have been inseparably, madly in love. In fact, a friend in college thought my last name was Nanna because he always heard, "Here comes Tim 'n Anna."

My love for Anna changed, though, as I sat all alone in a West Texas church. Although we had dated only a few months, I knew Anna was the one. But on that day, I was gripped with a strange fear of losing her. The service ended with *I Surrender All*, a hymn I had sung countless times. This time, though, it pierced my soul. I cried out in my spirit, "I surrender Anna to you, Lord. I don't know what that means, but she's yours." And instantly, my fear was replaced with the most surreal peace.

Turns out, that was just the first of many times I've had to surrender my greatest treasures to God. Surrender is never easy, but I've learned that victory starts with surrender, and surrender starts with submission. Anything worthwhile must be submitted to God. He is in control. He is Lord. And everything must be submitted to His lordship, even our relationships.

Ephesians 5 is controversial for people who reject a wife's submission to her husband's leadership. Yes, the three verses about wives' submission are hard, but the nine verses for men is an even higher bar of submission – to love his wife as Christ loved the church and gave His life for the church. Both examples of submission are possible when we "submit to one another out of reverence for Christ" (Eph. 5:21).

Sadly, we tend to have two extremes. We either act like an old boss of mine who would slam his fist and yell, "I'm in charge!" (Newsflash, the more you demand submission, the less you get it.) Or second, we passively abdicate our responsibility as servant-leaders and hope our family will somehow know how to submit biblically and want to. Both extremes are a disaster.

Don't demand submission; model it. Don't be weak; be meek (strength with control). Don't abdicate responsibility; take it. And the key to modeling meek, responsible submission is living out the three secrets of abiding relationships.

Three Secrets of Abiding Relationships:

1. Submit my wants to their needs

The first secret of abiding relationships is submitting my wants to the other person's needs. Ask: What will help them abide with God? Then submit to that need. Don't wait until you want to submit. Submit first, even if they don't reciprocate or thank you.

The key to joyful submission is remembering why you submit. You submit because it's what they need. It's a joyful gift you get to give, not a requirement you must give. Also, please don't bow to all their wants. Instead, surrender to their true needs. The only way to know what they need, though, is to become a student of what they need.

2. Study their needs

We wrongly assume that other people's needs are the same as ours. Thus, the second secret of abiding relationships is becoming a student of what they need – a combination of what God wants for all of us (Chapter 5 – Established identity) and God's unique mission for each of us (Chapter 8 – Transforming mission).

Becoming a submitting student of their needs enables us to accomplish the third secret of abiding relationships – the secret that grabs and holds their attention: serving their needs.

3. <u>Serve their needs</u>

The best leaders are the best servants. And the best servants help us meet our #1 need – to be faithful. That's what Jesus did. He served people's needs and showed them how by doing the lowly job of a slave – washing their feet (John 13:1-17). He didn't come to be served; he came to serve others and meet their need for a Savior (Matt. 20:28).

But we can't serve what we don't know. And we can't know what we don't understand. And we can't truly understand God's plan for abiding relationships unless we happily do whatever it takes to submit to other people's needs.

Healthy homes are submitting homes. Husbands to God. Wives to husbands. Kids to parents. Everyone to each other. Sorry, Disney, but this is the real "circle of life" – submitting to one another, which leads to studying one another, which leads to serving one another, which enables the next healthy habit of abiding relationships: loving and respecting each other.

#2 Love-respect

Give my love-respect; earn yours

Each one of you also must love his wife as he loves himself, and the wife must respect her husband. – Eph. 5:33

It's not until you become a parent that you realize how much parents give. I can see now how my mom gave me patience, love, and empathy. My dad gave me courage, work ethic, and tenacity. But my parents also gave me something far, far better that I call "give mine; earn yours." That is, they give love and respect to people whether they deserve it or not. And instead of demanding it in return, my parents try to earn it. Not as an exchange, but as a gift, no matter how they are treated.

Sadly, many people get it backwards. They live as if their motto is "give yours; earn mine." They demand that you to give them love and respect, while they require you to earn theirs. They complain, disrespect, and bark orders, and then wonder why people (especially their kids) don't respond well.

Love-respect is one word because it's intertwined like a chocolate-vanilla swirl cone. All of us need both love and respect, but just like how Anna wants more chocolate than vanilla, she needs extra love. And like most men, I need extra respect.

One of the best things about "give mine; earn yours" is that no one can stop you from giving love-respect, and no one can offend you by not giving it to you. It's a choice you make to bless others, like what God does for us. But for clarity, love-respect is often mistaken for something else: trust. And trust is earned. I don't have to trust you, but I can always love and respect you.

Healthy homes are built on love-respect. Healthy marriages too – a man loving his wife and a woman respecting her husband (Eph. 5:33). Here are eight keys for a loving, respectful marriage – five keys for him to give her what she needs most (love), and three keys for her to give him what he needs most (respect).

Five Keys to Love Your Wife:

1. Share your heart

A healthy man is both strong and transparent. He connects with her heart by sharing his, expecting nothing in return. For example (warning, it's about to get real), when did I buy flowers for Anna? It was when she was on her period, because I wasn't giving to get. I was giving to bring her joy. So, men, if you want a healthy home, love her no matter what, even if she doesn't love you back.

2. Sacrifice your treasures

The test of a healthy man isn't the dream he'll pursue to be happy; it's the dream he'll sacrifice to be faithful. Many men give their best at work but give leftovers at home. That's not love. Love sacrifices its treasures. Momma may never say it, but what she really wants is real sacrifice that flows from real love.

3. Surrender your pride

Let's face it, men are proud. Add to that a yearning for strength, power, and control, and it's no wonder many marriages struggle. Momma doesn't need her man to act like her in order to connect with her. She needs him to surrender his pride so that he never surrenders his love for her.

4. Shower your generosity

A healthy man lives in abundance, not scarcity. He doesn't hoard or hold back. He blesses his family by showering his wife with generosity in all areas. Not a sprinkling or spattering. It's a shower of agape love from which your family can drink.

5. Sharpen your bond

Like sharpening a pencil, healthy men have a point – love my kids well by loving my wife well. Don't just date her to marry her. Make her dreams come true with a godly man bonded to her through unwavering, unpretentious, uncompromising love.

Three Keys to Respect Your Husband:

1. Embrace the need

The question isn't if your husband deserves respect. It's if you'll embrace his need for respect. Sadly, many wives give respect as a reward for good behavior. Sure, he should treat you with the same respect he wants. But, ladies, if you want a healthy home, respect him anyway. No, that's not easy or fair, but that's love-respect.

2. Imagine the blessing

Respect imagines a better future. If your husband doesn't love you like you imagined, respect him like he never imagined. No matter how he responds, your respect will bless your kids with a transforming view of God and family.

3. Believe it is worth it

Respecting him doesn't guarantee that he'll love you. Not respecting him, though, nearly guarantees that he won't reciprocate. The key is softening him, not convincing him: "So that, if any of them do not believe the word, they may be won over without words by the behavior of their wives, when they see the purity and reverence in your lives" (1 Peter 3:1-2).

As the groom, Jesus didn't wait for His bride (the church) to act properly before giving His unconditional love and undeserved respect. He gave fully, joyfully, and continually, even when scorned and crucified, so that we too can live the next healthy habit of abiding relationships: forgiveness.

#3 Forgiveness

Show compassion by truly forgiving

Be kind and compassionate to one another, forgiving each other, just as in Christ God forgave you. – Eph. 4:32

Fool me once, shame on you. Fool me twice, shame on me. Fool me 77 times, forget shame . . . that's forgiveness. After all, it's hard to forgive more than once or twice. So, when Peter suggested that he forgive seven times, he was being generous.

Jesus' response, though, blew Peter away – forgive 77 times (Matt. 18:22). How in the world is that even possible? The only way is to abide in Jesus, the innocent lamb who died in our place to forgive our sins. In heaven, Jesus is our advocate, interceding for us (1 John 2:1, Rom. 8:34). And on earth, He prayed for His killers: "Father, forgive them, for they do not know what they are doing" (Luke 23:34).

A remarkable example of forgiveness is Ike Brown, whose son was murdered. Ike wanted to hate his son's killer, but he couldn't. Instead, Ike forgave his son's killer and later adopted him. Ike received the grace to love him and make him part of Ike's family – a vivid picture of what God does for us.

Forgiveness is a command, not a suggestion: "Be kind and compassionate to one another, forgiving each other, just as in Christ God forgave you" (Eph. 4:32). Compassion doesn't cling to bitterness because they can't coexist. But compassion and forgiveness always go together. You can't have one without the other. You can't turn the other cheek while harboring hate. And you can't blame it on not having the gift of mercy. I have a hard time spelling mercy, but God expects all of us to extend the mercy He gives us.

One day, a co-worker decided he'd had enough of me and said: "Did it ever cross your mind that all this faith stuff is just a pile of #$@?" Well, I don't recall my exact reply, but I was proud of what I didn't say . . . until three days later at church. It was like the preacher was looking right at me as he preached on forgiveness. Has that ever happened to you too?

Yes, my co-worker was wrong. But so was I. My words weren't harsh, but my heart was. So, the next day, I did what I had to do – apologize and ask for my co-worker's forgiveness. No, forgiving isn't fun, but it's the gateway to reconciliation. You can talk about compassion all day long, but compassion isn't kind without forgiveness.

Forgiveness says more about the forgiver than the forgiven. Even when people reject God's forgiveness, He still gives it. And so must we. Many Christians struggle with this because we struggle with our own guilt. Or we can't let go. Or we let it fester, causing spiritual ulcers. So, instead of trying to forget a sin against you, release it with four pursuits of forgiveness that honor God and build abiding relationships.

Four Pursuits of Forgiveness:

1. Pursue their mercy

Forgiveness starts with mercy – not getting what you deserve. And that happens when you pursue it, not by default. For example, when my integrity was falsely attacked, I wanted to lash out. But I had to realize that we all deserve judgment, not mercy. Thus, instead of wishing for God's justice on my accusers, I had to ask for God's richest mercy to cover them.

2. Pursue their grace

Forgiveness continues with grace – getting what you don't deserve. You can be gracious on the outside, yet bitter on the inside. The remedy for bitterness is praying a blessing of grace over them. You can't be bitter against someone while sincerely praying for them. It's not just being okay if God blesses them; it's asking God to shower them with blessings. "For in the same way you judge others, you will be judged, and with the measure you use, it will be measured to you" (Matt. 7:2).

3. Pursue their restoration

While my nature is to attack back, I'm learning to pursue forgiveness and restoration as God forgave and restored me (Col. 3:13). No matter the injustice, restored fellowship must be our goal (Matt 18:15). Restoration isn't keeping our distance; it's coming close to foster fellowship.

4. Pursue their joy

The result of God's mercy, grace, and restoration is joy. And joy is a choice, not a feeling, especially when we've been wronged. We want offenders to get justice, but God wants them to experience the joy of forgiveness.

Forgiveness is the best in you overlooking the worst in others. It isn't begrudging or partial. It's compassionate and consistent.

And although we struggle with "forgive and forget," God doesn't struggle. He forgives and forgets our sins if we confess them (Is. 43:25, Heb. 8:12). I don't understand that kind of compassion, but I can receive it and, in turn, pass it along through the next habit of abiding relationships: prayer.

#4 Prayer

Duct tape relationships with prayer

And pray in the Spirit on all occasions with all kinds of prayers and requests. With this in mind, be alert and always keep on praying for all the Lord's people. – Eph. 6:18

Is there anything duct tape can't fix? My son is obsessed with duct tape. He uses it to patch, seal, protect, and repair everything. It lasts forever, sticks to nearly anything, smooths rough edges, sizes to any situation, and even applies to sores.

That's what prayer is for relationships. It patches broken relationships, seals disconnected families, and protects against any problem. What are your rough edges? Use God's duct tape – prayer – to fix them. Do you have frayed, broken, or sore relationships? Let prayer patch them. Do you live with the constant dripping of lost personal connections? Pray for God to seal them. Pray persistently, continually, and gratefully (Luke 18:1, 1 Thess. 5:17, Phil. 4:6). Pray to prevent temptation, not just escape it (Matt. 26:41). Pray, knowing God listens and answers (Jer. 29:12, Ps. 17:6). Pray always for all people (Eph. 6:18).

Through prayer, I've seen terminal cancer disappear, shattered marriages reborn, prodigal children return, and frozen pipes melt. God uses prayer to duct tape everything, especially us.

Once, I shared the gospel with a couple who acted completely indifferent. Suddenly, as if a switch flipped, they prayed to receive Christ. When I got home, Anna asked me, "What happened at

7:43 tonight? At that moment, God told me to pray for you." Wow, I remembered looking at my watch at that exact time because it's when that couple's interest suddenly flipped.

My favorite duct-tape prayers came from my girls on my 57th birthday. I sensed that God wanted me to resign from being the Executive Pastor of my church, but it made no sense. I loved my church. We had just started a huge capital campaign. What would people say? How could the campaign happen without me? (I was wrong, but it's how I felt.) Then for the first time ever, our kids encircled Anna and me, laid hands on us, and prayed over us. They had no idea how I was struggling, but our girls' prayers on that birthday were like duct tape for my soul.

First, Emily prayed Jehovah Jireh over me. She didn't know I had wrestled with God that morning for an hour, begging for a deeper meaning of Jehovah Jireh – "God will provide." I wanted to trust Him to provide, but I didn't know how.

Second, Leslie prayed Psalm 119:105 over me. She had no idea that hours earlier I had told God that I needed Him to be a lamp to my feet and a light to my path (Psalm 119:105). Although I wanted a flashlight to see my exact path, I had prayed for help to trust Him to illuminate my next step, no matter where it led.

Third, Robyn prayed, "God, help Tim to not doubt in the dark what you reveal to him in the light." Robyn didn't know I was doubting what God had been showing me about resigning my Executive Pastor position. After all, I had surrendered my career to become a vocational minister, so what in the world would I do now? Who would hire a 57-year-old former CFO who left his Executive Pastor role without a "good reason"?

Yet again, prayer was God's duct tape in my life. My girls' prayers not only mirrored my prayers that morning, but they also revealed the three prayers we all can pray to trust God's faithfulness and praise Him in advance for the outcome.

Three Prayers of God's Faithfulness:

1. God will provide

When God told Abraham to sacrifice his son Isaac, it made no sense. Nevertheless, Abraham obeyed, God saved Isaac, and we learned a characteristic of Jehovah Jireh – God will provide (Gen. 22:14). Although this is a familiar story, it can be quite rare to see its message lived out: trust God to provide no matter what.

God does provide (Heb. 10:23). He does have a plan for us. And He does want the best for us (Jer. 29:11). He restores us (Jer. 30:17), pours out blessings on us (Mal. 3:10), and provides all our needs (Phil. 4:19). Even when we can't see His plan, we need to do what Emily prayed – trust Jehovah Jireh to provide.

2. God will guide

Jesus said we must come to Him like a little child (Matt. 18:3). I love it when my little grandkids hold my hand and trust me to guide and protect them. I won't steer them wrong.

So too, God won't leave us to wander aimlessly or steer us wrong. He doesn't just hope we'll figure it out. But He also doesn't give us GPS turn-by-turn directions. He does what Leslie prayed over me – He illumines our path. Not with a flashlight to see way out front, but with a lamp to take a next step of faith.

3. God is reliable

God never changes. He doesn't tune us out, have bad days, or need do-overs. He is reliable. But we must fully rely on Him and pray with right motives (James 4:2-3). If so, our prayers will be powerful and effective (James 5:16). Indeed, Robyn was right: Don't doubt in the dark what God reveals to you in the light.

Please take a moment to score the four healthy habits of A – Abiding relationships for you and your home. And please choose one of the four habits – Submission, Love-respect, Forgiveness, or Prayer – that you most want to grow.

<u>Abiding Relationships</u>   <u>You</u> Home

<u>Submission</u>: *Submit my wants to your needs*   ___ ___
<u>Love-respect</u>: *Give my love-respect; earn yours*   ___ ___
<u>Forgiveness</u>: *Show compassion by truly forgiving*   ___ ___
<u>Prayer</u>: *Duct tape relationships with prayer*   ___ ___

Total   ___ ___

/4 = Average   ☐ ☐

The Abiding relationships habit I'll grow is: _____

Exercise: "Agape Qualities"

How agape is my love, really?

My friend, David Ingram, absolutely loves God's Word. The Bible is the filter through which David sees life and the roadmap that guides his steps. And David's favorite Bible word is agape – the unconditional, abounding, unending, selfless love of Jesus. It's how Jesus loves us and the reciprocal love that we must have for Him and each other.

There's nothing like agape love. It frees us up to live a whole new world of joy, not just happiness. It enlightens and lifts burdens. It creates security and peace in the darkest days. And it builds boundaries that protect and bridges that connect.

But the best way to know if you're living with agape isn't the way I describe it. It's the way God describes it. Below are sixteen agape qualities from the "love chapter" of 1 Corinthians 13. In this exercise, please pick three of the sixteen that are your best agape qualities and three that are your weakest. Don't rank or score them. Just place a check mark by your Top 3 and your Bottom 3.

Agape Qualities	Top 3	Bottom 3
1. I am patient.	___	___
2. I am kind.	___	___
3. I am not jealous.	___	___
4. I do not brag or boast.	___	___
5. I am not arrogant or proud.	___	___
6. I am not rude or dishonoring.	___	___
7. I am not self-seeking or selfish.	___	___
8. I am not easily angered or provoked.	___	___
9. I do not act resentful or consider wrongs.	___	___
10. I am not glad about sin or injustice.	___	___
11. I rejoice with the truth.	___	___
12. I bear and protect all things (like a roof).	___	___
13. I believe and trust all things.	___	___
14. I hope and am confident in all things.	___	___
15. I endure and persevere in all things.	___	___
16. My love does not fail or fall away.	___	___

What are your Top 3? Your Bottom 3?

My Top 3 are #11, 12, and 15. My Bottom 3 are #1, 8, and 9. I need to be more patient, unfazed, and unresentful, but agape love is a journey with many missteps. So, we need to keep walking, keep growing, and keep abiding in faith, hope, and agape love. "But the greatest of these is (agape) love" (1 Cor. 13:13).

Since your family's relationships with God likely look much like your relationships with them, they need to see agape love flow from you. And they can when you know who God is (H), what God says about you (E), and how to connect with God and others (A). The next step of a HEALTHY home builds the credibility to help your family become receptive to your faith: Legacy disciplines – all the little disciplines that add up to a godly legacy.

Chapter 7

Big Rock #4:

L – Legacy Disciplines

Healthy disciplines
create godly legacies

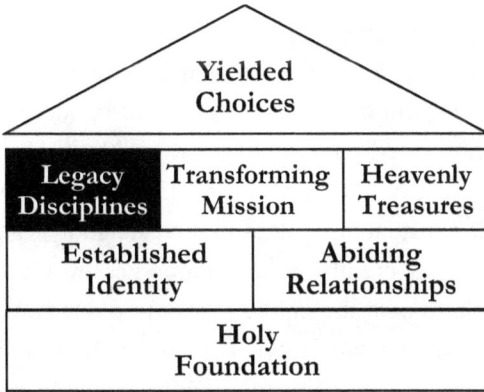

	Yielded Choices		
Legacy Disciplines	Transforming Mission		Heavenly Treasures
Established Identity		Abiding Relationships	
Holy Foundation			

Protect your house
with plenty of *insulation*

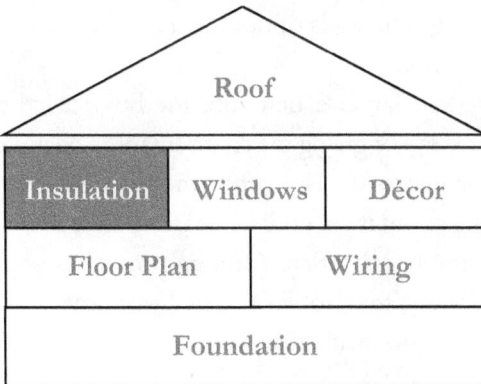

	Roof		
Insulation	Windows		Décor
Floor Plan		Wiring	
Foundation			

After building a house's foundation, framing it by following the floor plan, and wiring it to the power source, make sure to protect it with plenty of insulation. All those little particles of insulation combine to prevent pipes from freezing, save energy, and build a defensive barrier against external forces.

Life is much the same. We need life disciplines to insulate our family from freezing up, wasting energy, and losing to external forces. No one life discipline by itself is enough, but a disciplined life forms a strong protective barrier.

Life disciplines involve personal discipline (self-control) and success disciplines (doing the things unhealthy people won't do). Both are crucial, but our dream goes beyond a successful legacy.

Our dream is a legacy of spiritual health. Therefore, please don't skimp on the "L" big rock of HEALTHY: *Legacy disciplines* – all the little spiritual disciplines that create godly legacies.

By creating a credibility that embodies everything we do, legacy disciplines earn the right to speak into our family's choices and insulate them from harm. And when all our little legacy disciplines match our big mission, we build on-ramps of receptivity and we tear down walls of resistance.

Sadly, there's no convenient time to add legacy disciplines. We get busy, don't feel like it, or forget. And no matter how well we insulate our family, we need more because they're always listening through the walls of our life. Here's a work example that illustrated this point.

On my first day at a new job, my boss called me into his office. But instead of giving me an orientation, he just complained about my predecessor. The problem was that my predecessor knew nothing about it . . . until he heard it while listening through the wall of my boss' office. Although my boss shouldn't have blabbed so loudly, the problem started years earlier with builders who cut corners on insulation.

We know we shouldn't cut corners, but sometimes we do because the effects aren't always obvious. For example, when we moved into a house 25 years ago, the prior owner didn't turn off the cable TV. While I love a freebie, I soon realized that it was a test of my character, and my family was watching. Would I skimp on the integrity I had preached, or would I be someone they could be proud of?

Is your family proud of the little things you do? Or do life's "little tests" disqualify your witness? Paul's advice on not disqualifying yourself is to be disciplined in the disciplines that keep you under control (1 Cor. 9:24-27). And it's the little things that often determine the legacy you pass down. Four of those legacy disciplines in Ephesians are: balance humility and conviction, be patient, preserve unity, and gush with gratitude.

Humble conviction	*Balance humility & conviction*
Patience	*To win the war, learn to wait*
Unity	*Turn conflicts into unifying "wows!"*
Gratitude	*Gush with gratitude*

Who do you know that is faithful in little things (Luke 16:10)? One of the finest examples I know is the family of Don and Elizabeth O'Neal. A fellow CEO asked Don for the one thing that caused his company to be so successful. Don's reply: "There is no silver bullet. It's simply doing all the little things a little better every day."

The O'Neal family also epitomizes spiritual health because they strive to do all the little disciplines a little better every day. Generations of their family have been filled with the Spirit and bear the fruit of the Spirit because they live their mission: "To serve others with excellence" (based on Colossians 3:23). And so can you if you'll do the legacy disciplines that unhealthy people won't do, starting with humble conviction.

#1 Humble Conviction

Balance humility and conviction

Be completely humble and gentle. – Eph. 4:2a

In him and through faith in him we may approach God with freedom and confidence. – Eph. 3:12

I know, I know. Once you think you're humble, you're not. Humility is a prize pursued, not possessed. But it's key to your family being receptive to God. Humility is disarming and heart-warming. It opens doors and mends fences. Humility isn't a side dish; it's a main dish that goes with everything.

The fruit of the Spirit passage starts with "serve one another humbly in love" (Gal 5:13b) and ends with "let us not be conceited" (Gal 5:26). The fruit itself – love, joy, peace, forbearance, kindness, goodness, faithfulness, gentleness, and self-control – is like the meat of a sandwich, with humility as the bread that holds it all together and adds flavor.

"In humility value others above yourselves" (Phil. 2:3). "Whoever takes the lowly position of this child is the greatest in the kingdom of heaven" (Matt. 18:4). "For those who exalt themselves will be humbled" (Matt. 23:12a).

Humility, though, is often misunderstood. It isn't weakness. Humility is a posture of outward service built on a position of inner strength. It doesn't crumble or capitulate. It raises the bar of excellence, not 10th place ribbons. But humility isn't enough.

Humility must be melded with conviction to form "humble conviction" – one healthy habit with two complementary parts. Don't choose between the two because God wants both – gentle humility (Eph. 4:2a) and confident freedom (Eph. 3:12).

If your humility exceeds your conviction, you aim too low. But if conviction exceeds humility, your message gets lost. Both imbalances miss the mark. When balanced and interwoven, though, they combine to create a godly passion that helps your family embrace humble conviction as their own.

Humility and conviction aren't incongruent; they're two sides of a coin. On one side, we humbly serve; on the other, we stay on task. Both caring and committed. Like the Apostle Paul, we can be both the "chief of sinners" and someone to imitate (1 Tim. 1:15, 1 Cor. 11:1).

By being a balance of unassuming and unwavering, you help your family believe in you and bond with you, so that they'll want to extend and expand your legacy of faithfulness. This godly passion opens their hearts to everything else you hope to see in them. And it helps them walk the balance beam of humble conviction without falling off on either side.

Two of my favorite examples of humble conviction are my sister, Sharon, and my friend, Steve LaMar. Sharon's unique blend of engaging humility and unshakable conviction helps her laugh at challenges that would crush most people. And while Steve is a fireball of hilarious sarcasm, he's also an inspiring, dedicated servant. Sharon and Steve are ordinary people who bless others in extraordinary ways because they live with godly passion. Here are three proofs of how you can do the same.

Three Proofs of Godly Passion:

1. A quest with a zest

Humble conviction has a quest with a zest that is deep down in you, not beat down into you. A quest is what you're called to do; a zest, what you're compelled to do with enthusiasm. Quest fills you up; zest fires you up. Together, they create a godly passion that's courageous and contagious, much like Sharon, Steve, and the O'Neals. The good news is that anyone, including you, can have godly passion. Who do you know like that?

2. **Desperation for God**

Humble conviction consumes you with a desperation for God. It's a willingness to sacrifice and an insistence upon sacrificing because you're desperate to experience Him. Whatever consumes you in private will eventually compel you in public. King David said, "Zeal for Your house consumes me" (Ps. 69:9). We're all consumed with something, but are you consumed with what consumes God?

3. **A teachable teacher**

People with godly passion are teachable teachers – willing and able to be taught as well as teach others. As recipients of God's grace and receptacles of His power, they can join Paul in saying, "The things you have heard me say in the presence of many witnesses entrust to reliable people who will also be qualified to teach others" (2 Tim. 2:2). How about you? What are you learning? And who are you teaching?

God favors those who humbly kneel and confidently pray in His name according to His will (James 1:6-8). That's a coin you can't spend on earth, but you can deposit it into your family and see it draw interest. And that requires patience.

#2 Patience

To win the war, learn to wait

Be patient, bearing with one another in love. – Eph. 4:2b

In our immediate-gratification society, be a crockpot. Not a microwave. More than ever, families need patience – the fourth fruit of the Spirit (Gal. 5:22) and the first quality of love: "Love is patient" (1 Cor. 13:4). Then again, patience is often the difference between a failed family and a faithful family.

Patience is like a behind-the-scenes character actor that helps your family win Best Picture. You may not notice it when it's done well, but it's obvious when done poorly.

The problem with patience is that it requires waiting, and I'd rather hear, "No!" than wait in silence. Sometimes it seems as if God is giving us the silent treatment. But God isn't ignoring us. He's getting us ready. "Let us not become weary in doing good, for at the proper time we will reap a harvest if we do not give up" (Gal. 6:9). "The testing of your faith produces (patience). Let (patience) finish its work so that you may be mature and complete, not lacking anything" (James 1:3-4).

Another problem with patience is that so few of us are good at it. Maybe that's why we get so many opportunities to practice it. And we must practice it because everyone needs it.

Patience is also hard because it requires action, not feelings. If you wait to be patient until you feel like it, you'll never get there. Don't blame your nature. Don't sit idly, expecting God to drop a solution in your lap. Receive the Spirit's gift of patience and live it. Then pray for feelings to follow.

Patience is a war with many battles. And unfortunately, I approached it wrong for years. I fought every little battle. While it's great to consistently instill faithfulness in the little things, what my family needed even more from me was patience. After all, the goal is to win the war for your family's souls, not fight every little battle. Here are five steps to help.

Five Steps to Win Your Family's Soul:

1. To win the war, win the right battles (Strategic)

You can't win the war without winning battles, but not every battle is worth winning. A clean bedroom is good, but not at the cost of nearly losing a daughter. Every pea isn't worth eating. Every attitude isn't worth fixing. Don't waver on spiritual disciplines and character, but don't lose relationships over battles that aren't strategic in winning their souls.

2. <u>To win the right battles, win their hearts</u>   (Connected)

Early on, you might win battles due to positional authority. But winning the right battles over the long haul requires you to win their hearts, which requires you to connect with their hearts. It shows that you care. They won't always agree, but they need alignment through connection. Not agreement through coercion.

3. <u>To win their hearts, earn their trust</u>   (Trustworthy)

You'll win their hearts with connection and care, but they have to trust you. I've heard that the first question people ask themselves about people they meet is: "Can I trust you?" And even after they know you, they keep asking that question. It's the same with families. Your family is routinely sizing up your trustworthiness because if they don't trust you, they won't hear you.

4. <u>To earn their trust, learn to listen</u>   (Present)

Trust isn't earned until people feel heard. They need you to listen intently and be present emotionally. Being present is my daughter's superpower. When Leslie is with you, she's *with you*, hearing all you say and feeling all you feel. And like her Lord, you can feel Leslie's presence even if you can't see her. That's why I'm invited to attend a lot of weddings, but Leslie is invited to be *in* a lot of weddings.

5. <u>To learn to listen, practice waiting</u>   (Patient)

Learning to listen comes from patiently waiting. Patience may not be your strength either, but if you want to win your family's soul, then fight the right battles, win their hearts, earn their trust, learn to listen, and practice waiting. But patience is where it starts. Patience is also the bridge to the next legacy discipline: Unity.

#3 Unity

Turn conflicts into unifying "wows!"

Make every effort to keep the unity of the Spirit through the bond of peace. There is one body and one Spirit, just as you were called to one hope when you were called. – Eph. 4:3-4

Conflict happens. And when it does, what do you do? Defer? Die on principle? Defend yourself? Demand you're right? I used to do virtually anything to avoid conflict, but not anymore. Because the one thing I hate more than conflict is the results of not dealing with it.

Since conflict is inevitable, I'm learning to navigate it by focusing on the right goal and doing my part. "Keep the unity of the Spirit through the bond of peace" (Eph. 4:3) and "If it is possible, as far as it depends on you, live at peace with everyone" (Rom. 12:18). Unity (aka peace) is so important, it's the third fruit of the Spirit in Galatians 5.

The goal of unity isn't fixing people. It's finding common ground that wins them over to faithfulness (Matt. 18:15). If God is both the author and the audience of your response to conflict, you've done your part for unity.

For example, although I absolutely love my church, our people, and our ministries, it hasn't always been easy. Decades ago, while navigating some church conflicts, I received legal threats, physical threats, and more. Still, it's a privilege to serve my church because, like a biological family, a church family can struggle. But that's okay because a church is family, and God's goal for His family is unity. You're not creating unity; you're just preserving the unity that God already created.

Unity is based on your position with God, not whether or not you agree on a position. I don't always like God's will, but I must align with it. So too, I don't have to agree with you to have unity

81

with you. I once told a friend, "It's okay if we don't agree, because it's okay if you're wrong." We could laugh about it because we understood Proverbs 27:17 – "As iron sharpens iron, so one person sharpens another."

At CiCi's Pizza, I learned to see conflict differently – as an opportunity to turn conflicts into unifying "wows!" When we turned a guest complaint into a wow or when guests called corporate to praise our people, we rang a big bell. But seriously, who hangs up from a complaint call feeling like a million bucks? And who calls corporate to praise someone? Nobody, right? Well, that bell rang often because our goal was to turn negatives into "wows!"

Instead of just managing family's conflicts, why not use them as opportunities to unify your family? What if you rang a unity bell when your kids praised each other? Even better than ringing a bell to celebrate unity, though, is understanding what prevents unity in the first place. So, let's review four approaches that *prevent* unity.

Four Approaches That Prevent Unity:

1. Capitulation (Lose/win)

Unity is not capitulation – deferring conflict in hopes that it goes away. That's lose/win . . . I lose so that you'll win and be happy. But being a doormat isn't unity. That's not turning the other cheek or walking an extra mile (Matt. 5:39, 41). That's just a subtle version of being a victim.

2. Superiority (Win/Lose)

Unity isn't the opposite of capitulation – superiority. That's win/lose. I win; you lose. It might deter conflict like how a strong military can deter war, but superiority is a horrible approach for families. It kicks the can down the road until "inferior" people get strong enough to fight back. Even if you win, your family loses.

3. <u>Absence of conflict</u> (Temporary Win/Win)

Unity is not the absence of conflict – delaying the inevitable. That's a temporary win/win. Conflict simmers and eventually boils over. You can't shake up your family like a soda can and expect them to not spew. Instead, ensure that any absence of conflict is peace, not a sink hole of conflict waiting to collapse.

4. <u>Consensus</u> (Illusionary Win/Win)

Finally, unity isn't consensus if it's only an illusionary win/win. Don't get lulled into feeling great because no one is disagreeing. Go-along-to-get-along is peer pressure – a festering cancer, not unified hearts. Consensus can be great, though, if it's aligned with God's heart because unified hearts result in the legacy discipline of gushing with gratitude.

#4 Gratitude

Gush with gratitude

Always giving thanks to God the Father for everything, in the name of our Lord Jesus Christ. – Eph. 5:20

Is there a more thankless job than parenting? We're glad to do it because we love them and want the best for them. Anna and I drove all over for our kids, spent a fortune, and lost sleep to support them. As do you.

But it's hard to be thankful when it feels thankless. Sassy attitudes are cute in infants, but not from entitled teenagers. And a newlywed's quirks soon stop being adorable. A lack of thanks turns into a thankless job unless you have the attitude of "it's my pleasure" and "it's my privilege."

For example, I love Chick-Fil-A's reply to everything: "My pleasure." It's great because they mean it. No eye rolls. No indifference. Just a joyful heart of service. It's living like my friend

Randy Draper, whose motto is: "Happy to do it!" Consistently. Immediately. Joyfully. Wholeheartedly.

The other part of gratitude – "it's my privilege" – reflects the honor of serving. For decades, my email salutation was: "Never forgetting the privilege of serving Him." I didn't always feel that way, but it often kept me from hitting send. How can I say it's a privilege to serve Him if I'm not serving you? Committing to that standard is hard, but the alternative is even worse – aiming for an easy standard that doesn't amount to much.

Gratitude is a gift you give God and people. Does your gratitude make it easy for your family to be grateful? "Whatever you do, whether in word or deed, do it all in the name of the Lord Jesus, giving thanks to God the Father through him" (Col. 3:17). "Give thanks in all circumstances; for this is God's will for you in Christ Jesus" (1 Thes. 5:18). "Give thanks to the LORD, for he is good; his love endures forever" (Ps. 106:1).

According to Ephesians 5:20, we should be grateful for everything. But is that really possible? Absolutely. I know a little girl who inspired thousands while battling cancer. A friend fought for a decade to pay massive debts because God told him to avoid bankruptcy. A co-worker oozed joy while her son languished in jail. They weren't always happy, but their goal wasn't happiness. Their goal was joy – the second fruit of the Spirit.

Moving from ungrateful to grateful is a progression, so we should break it up into three COW's – chunks of work. Each COW is a milestone that mooooves us closer to the source of true joy – gushing with gratitude.

Three Milestones of Gratitude:

1. Receptive hearts
The first milestone of gratitude is receptivity – willing to listen. If you want your family to have a willing-to attitude, be willing to listen, learn, and lead by example. You don't have to agree with

them, but you need to listen and understand. Don't force them to drink from your well; lead them to drink like a deer panting for God's well of living water (Ps. 42:1, John 4:10).

2. Responsive hearts

Willingness is worthless without responsiveness – wanting to act. Don't just tell your family what to do; show them. Turn good intentions into good works. Like the first part of a spiritually healthy home ("help your family want"), create a want-to of responsiveness that turns hearers into doers (James 1:22).

3. Rejoicing hearts

The final milestone of gratitude is rejoicing – choosing to praise. "Rejoice in the Lord always. I will say it again: Rejoice!" (Phil. 4:4). When entrenched religious leaders complained to Jesus about people praising Him as the Messiah, Jesus replied, "If they keep quiet the stones will cry out" (Luke 19:40). Make sure that the stones never have to cry out in your home. And if you'll keep rejoicing, they won't have to. Then again, I've never met anyone who wished their family was less joyful.

My kids learned early on that entitlement got them nowhere with me, but gratitude opened the floodgates of generosity. I want them to be more than just thankful. I pray they'll have a sustained gratitude bubbling forth from a sustained relationship with Jesus. It might seem like a little thing, but a grateful heart forms a rock-solid barrier of protection that will insulate your home and outlive you for generations to come.

Please take a moment to score these four healthy habits of L – Legacy disciplines for you and your home. And note which of the four healthy habits you want most to grow – Humble conviction, Patience, Unity, or Gratitude.

Legacy Disciplines	You	Home
Humble conviction: *Balance humility & conviction*	___	___
Patience: *To win the war, learn to wait*	___	___
Unity: *Turn conflicts into unifying "wows!"*	___	___
Gratitude: *Gush with gratitude*	___	___
Total	___	___
/4 = Average	☐	☐

The Legacy disciplines habit I'll grow is: _____

Another great legacy discipline to instill in your family is being a serial encourager. No special skill or anointing is required. Anyone can do it. And when it's given with no string attached, encouragement can change eternity. Here's an exercise called "Reasons I Love You" to take encouragement to another level.

Exercise: "Reasons I Love You"

Encourage the best in others

As shared in *Well Done, Mom & Dad!*, the first time I did this exercise was on our 50th birthday (yes, Anna and I have the same birthday . . . I'm four hours older). I gave her a list called *50 Reasons It's a Privilege to be Your Husband* – a compilation of her best qualities, fond memories, inside jokes, and more. Anna absolutely loved it. But I wasn't trying to impress her; just encourage her.

I know that Anna feels loved, but she also loved reading why I love her. Plus, articulating these reasons forced me to think through why she's so special. And what did my kids do in response? Much to my surprise, on Fathers' Day, they gave me their own list: *50 Reasons You Are an Awesome Father.*

I was blown away. Turns out, my kids loved seeing their mom encouraged, and they wanted the same for me. Some of their 50 reasons were big events, but most were little everyday choices that became big things as they grew older, such as taking them to church every week, laughing over meals, and loving their mom.

And while I loved reading about my kids' favorite childhood memories, I was blessed even more by something I saw a decade later at my son's house – a list titled *36 Reasons I Love You*. When I asked Caleb about it, he said, "Yeah, Dad, I took a page out of your playbook and gave Emily this list on her 36th birthday."

I'm not bragging at all because our family has challenges too. But we're committed to doing "little" disciplines that connect and keep us vulnerable with each other and God. And we try to encourage each other in little things that take root and sometimes sprout years later.

Creating a "Reasons I Love You" list is simple. Just articulate why you love your spouse, family member, friend, co-worker, neighbor, minister, or anyone you want to bless. It might be on a birthday, anniversary, Christmas, or New Years Day. I like to type lists, but you might prefer a handwritten note or video.

Consider getting away together to share the stories behind your "reasons." You might plan quality time to unpack your reasons. Or you might discuss them while serving people in need. The key, though, is communicating why you love them in personal ways that connect with them.

For illustrative purposes, here's an updated list I gave Anna on our 60th birthday.

Sixty Reasons It's a Privilege to Be Your Husband

1. Leslie, Joshua & Caleb	2. Your heart still skips a beat
3. My best friend	4. Salado
5. Always believing in me	6. Sweet, kind spirit
7. Unquestioned loyalty	8. Encouragement
9. Fun	10. Hugs
11. Patience	12. Choosing the library

13. Back scratches
14. "Is this the Trevi Fountain?"
15. Molokai mule rides
16. Caring for our parents
17. Master of simple recipes
18. Skiing slow
19. A true servant-leader
20. Being grateful
21. Praising & obeying God
22. Choosing to choose
23. Laughing at my jokes
24. Being a China doll
25. Completing me
26. Loving me more than chocolate
27. Modeling true generosity
28. Oozing true humility
29. Integrity above reproach
30. Saying, "Enough" when needed
31. Living a godly legacy
32. Respecting me no matter what
33. Refusing to fight
34. Getting angry only 2 ½ times
35. Being our family's glue
36. Making bonding memories
37. Humoring Vacation Tim
38. Loving other people's children
39. Watching guy movies
40. Pursuing real life in Christ
41. Praying for our family
42. Trusting my judgment
43. "Good thing I'm cute"
44. "Gotta love me"
45. Making me smell the roses
46. Helping me pursue my dreams
47. Being authentic
48. Hurting with people who hurt
49. Aging gracefully
50. Being GrAnna
51. Endless banners
52. Surviving the Drake Passage
53. Forgiving quickly
54. Letting me kill your spiders
55. 9 Christmas stockings
56. Hosing off Josh's little hiney
57. In 'n Out & Andy's
58. 38 great years + 3 bonus years
59. Living "Well done!"
60. Our kids are your vow (Prov. 3:2)

Sharing why you love people not only encourages them, but it also opens their hearts to the "T" of a HEALTHY home – Transforming mission, the big rock that helps turn *your* legacy into *their* legacy, albeit in their own unique ways.

Chapter 8

Big Rock #5:

T – Transforming Mission

Healthy missions
transform your world

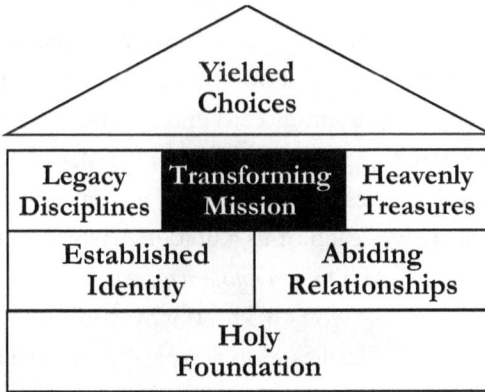

	Yielded Choices	
Legacy Disciplines	Transforming Mission	Heavenly Treasures
Established Identity		Abiding Relationships
Holy Foundation		

Enlighten your house
with *windows*

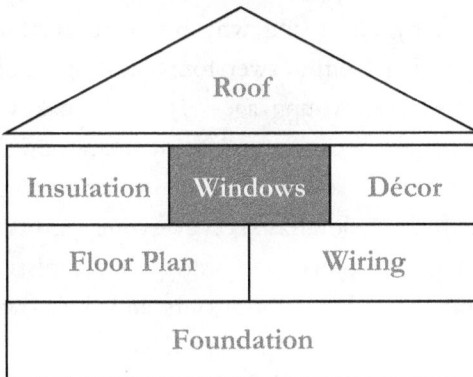

	Roof	
Insulation	Windows	Décor
Floor Plan		Wiring
Foundation		

Now that your house is framed, wired, and insulated, it needs windows. By adding light and warmth, windows make rooms seem bigger. They bring energy, improve your mood, and help you get beyond your little world and see what awaits outside.

Like house windows, you need spiritual windows to allow spiritual light into your home. Spiritual windows enlighten, warm, and help you get outside yourself to see a big God with a big mission for you. But are you *instilling* (inspiring) spiritual light into your family, or *installing* (pushing) spiritual light on them?

That is, are you helping them discover their own unique mission, or trying to pick it for them? As a steward of your family's eternity, help them discern and embrace "an inheritance that can never perish, spoil or fade" (1 Pet. 1:4).

While God creates all of us with a common established identity, He also gives each of us a unique personal mission – the "T" big rock of HEALTHY: *Transforming mission.*

Mission is key for you to know why you exist and where you're going. Still, families don't typically get excited about mission . . . unless it's personal, fun, and discovered together. A mission needs to be a blend of believability (close enough to reality) and growth (what you want to become), and it must be uniquely you. For example, here's how my family did it.

We started by discussing why we were creating a family mission and having them answer four questions that resonated with my kids at their young ages: 1) What makes our family unique? 2) What are your favorite family memories? 3) What are your favorite Christian songs? 4) What are your favorite verses?

I wrote a draft version based on everyone's answers and then we refined it together. Since the resulting family mission included everyone's input, it felt like both ours and their own. And it's uniquely us – a *Declaration of Him-dependence.*

On signature day, I got parchment paper, a huge white feather pen, a black robe, and a 1776-looking curly white wig. We also took photos and put them in a huge frame next to our signed family declaration. Our declaration created great conversations with guests but, far better, it created indelible memories for our family because it was a promise we made together . . . a promise to God of what matters most to us – depending on Him.

For a mission to transform your future, though, it must also keep renewing your mind so that you can know God's "good, pleasing and perfect will" (Rom. 12:2). Life transformation is the proof, but it's made possible by knowing what success looks like and clearly articulating it, wholeheartedly obeying it, and missionally living it.

Success	*Know God's calling for you*
Clarity	*Never live in the shadows of vague*
Obedience	*Obey wholeheartedly, not compliantly*
Missional	*Live for your mission, not your methods*

A transforming mission should be prominently displayed as a visual reminder. But more importantly, your mission must hang on your hearts, not just your walls. It should reflect your heart, stir your memories, and transform you into God's image (2 Cor. 3:18). Therefore, every family member needs to help create it. Then it becomes a tool to create a renewing family with a pure, steadfast spirit (Ps. 51:10).

A transforming mission also needs tangible expressions – the "real life" of my church's mission: "Real people. Real hope. Real life." We're not perfect people, but we have real life because our hope in Christ is transforming us. Then again, your mission isn't a reality until your family knows it's real.

But first, ask yourself: Do I know my mission? Does my family know? You may think your mission is transforming, but is it really? A transforming mission starts with knowing and fulfilling God's calling for you – the healthy habit of success.

#1 Success

Know God's calling for you

Making the most of every opportunity, because the days are evil. –
Eph. 5:16

As a prisoner for the Lord, then, I urge you to live a life worthy of
the calling you have received. – Eph. 4:1

Everyone wants success. So, why is success so elusive? Maybe it's
due to a lack of self-discipline or a struggle with procrastination,
toxic habits, or poor physical health. Or maybe we aim for the
wrong things. Many times, though, we lack success because we've
never taken time to think through what it looks like. And success
in tasks can be clear, but success in life is far less obvious.

God's view of success for you is His target for you. But you
have to know God's target – His calling – for you because you
can't fulfill what you don't know. Regardless of your specific
calling, I believe success has two parts:

1) Maximize your opportunity – "making the most of every
   opportunity" (Eph. 5:16) and
2) Be faithful today – "live a life worthy of the calling you
   have received" (Eph. 4:1).

It's a vision for tomorrow and an action for today. An
ultimate mission with an urgent mandate. Knowing God's path
and taking steps to walk it. Both strategic and tactical.

My definition of success isn't necessarily better than yours,
but it's biblical, deeply personal, and my filter for life. It's how
God wired me and His target for me. But what is God's target of
success for you? Can you succinctly describe it? In her classic
book *What MORE Can I Say?*, Dianna Booher notes, "If you can't
write it in a sentence, you can't say it in an hour."

No matter how you describe success, what matters is what God says about it. And God measures success not by the comparability of your accomplishments, but by the completeness of your faithfulness.

Success doesn't guarantee a great result, but it maximizes the opportunity God gives you. It plants God's seeds in God's way, for God's pleasure, and trusts God with the result. Here are six seeds of success, including three to maximize your opportunity and three to be faithful today.

Three Seeds to Maximize Your Opportunity:

1. Grow from yesterday's setbacks

We learn more from setbacks than successes. My family wanted to know about my setbacks because they gained hope in knowing what I overcame to get here. So, instead of cowering from, or covering up, your setbacks, use them as a launching pad to maximize your opportunity.

2. See beyond today's possibilities

Successful families see beyond today. Like God, they see what you can be. God saw David's heart, not his flaws. He saw Moses' leadership, not his speech impediment. He saw Saul as the Apostle Paul, not a terrorist. What do you imagine God sees in you and your family? No matter your current situation, God sees you as a priceless pottery of possibilities to mold for His glory.

3. Strain toward tomorrow's prize

"One thing I do: forgetting what is behind and straining toward what is ahead, I press on toward the goal to win the prize for which God has called me heavenward in Christ Jesus" (Phil. 3:13-14). Like Paul, don't strain for accomplishments; strain for the heavenly prize of walking worthy of your calling.

Three Seeds to Be Faithful Today:

1. Become a character hero

More than stellar results, families need stellar character. And since you are the primary source of your family's character, you need to be a character hero who instills character in them, speaks character over them, and celebrates the character already within them. This chapter's exercise can help you choose the character qualities that will make you a family hero for eternity.

2. Grow into a servant-leader

Character heroes grow into servant-leaders. They learn to serve their God-honoring purpose by serving others. They don't just agree to serve; they strive to serve. And they don't drag you; they lead you to become a servant-leader too. Service earns the right to lead, which leads to being faithful today.

3. Fulfill your mission

When God reveals His mission for you, take action. Don't wait until you understand it all. Sprint to fulfill what you know. There's nothing more rewarding than fulfilling your mission. And there's nothing more powerful for your family than to see you fulfilling a transforming mission that you articulate with clarity.

#2 Clarity

Never live in the shadows of vague

To make plain to everyone the administration of this mystery, which for ages past was kept hidden in God, who created all things. – Eph. 3:9

Unless you clearly know what success looks like, you'll live in the shadows, never knowing if you're successful. This became clear to me while watching (of all things) the James Bond movie, *Skyfall.* When Agent 007's boss said, "We can't keep working in the shadows," it was as if God said, "Tim, stop living in the shadows of vague."

Vagueness leads to mediocrity and confusion. As Dianna Booher puts it: "It's difficult to lead people to a place they cannot see, to an understanding you yourself do not have, or to a goal you cannot communicate."

But don't just talk about a family mission; put it in writing. "Make plain" your calling and "live a life worthy" of that calling (Eph. 3:9, 4:1). If you can't make it plain, how can your family understand it? Written family missions build accountability and buy in by building a common language, common expectations, and common passion that they'll talk about for years.

Even if clarity seems unnecessary because it's obvious to you, your family needs it. About the time you get tired of talking about your mission, they'll start getting it. Like an onion, each layer of clarity may bring a tear to your eye and a jolt to your senses, but it gets you down to the good parts that flavor everything.

So, what should you clarify? Everything! Clarify your love for your family, your commitment to them, and your prayers over them. Clarify your relationship with God, calling from Him, and hope due to Him. Clarify the fullness found in Him. Clarify your successes and trials. Clarify it all because they want to know it all.

By clearly articulating our mission, we model God's example. God used 40 people to clarify His mission in 66 books over 1,500 years. Without this clarity, we'd lack confidence in Him. What if Paul didn't clarify how to walk in Christ? What if Matthew, Mark, Luke, and John didn't articulate Jesus' words and deeds? Without John's Revelation, how would we know that we win in the end?

An unclear mission is like the game called "gossip," where everyone sits in a circle, and the first person whispers something to the second person, who whispers it to the third, and so on. By the time it goes around the room, the original message gets lost because it was passed along without clarity. Don't let that be your family. Give them the advantages of a crystal-clear mission.

Four Advantages of Crystal Clarity:

1. End uncertainty

Without clarity, people stress and financial markets crash. With clarity, though, they flourish because clarity brings certainty. Even bad news is better than vague news because you can adapt if you know what to expect. No matter how crazy life gets, the certainty of God's love will brighten your soul.

2. Reveal light

Dark and light can't coexist because light always wins. Clarity is a light that illuminates darkness and reveals the truth that Jesus is "the light of the world. Whoever follows me will never walk in darkness, but will have the light of life" (John 8:12). By clarifying biblical truth, the enemy will scatter (Ps. 68:1) like a cockroach that runs away from light.

3. Build trust

When you lose trust, you lose the ability to lead. And a great way to build trust is to be crystal clear in what you expect of yourself, which lets your family know what to expect of you, which lets you be clear in what you expect of them. Little nuggets of clarity not only help them trust you, but also help them trust God.

4. Create alignment

With a little clarity, your family can know enough to accept what you want. With more clarity, they might agree. And with much clarity comes alignment with your mission, but with a caveat: your character must align with your mission. That is: Clear mission + Clear character = Clear alignment. And clear alignment with God's will significantly increases the likelihood of family success as long as you're obedient.

#3 Obedience

Obey wholeheartedly, not compliantly

Obey them not only to win their favor when their eye is on you, but as slaves of Christ, doing the will of God from your heart. Serve wholeheartedly, as if you were serving the Lord, not people, because you know that the Lord will reward each one for whatever good they do. – Eph. 6:6-8

Do not be foolish, but understand what the Lord's will is. – Eph. 5:17

How do you like it when someone tells you what to do? Even if they're right, you want to push back, correct? As a kid, I hated being told to obey my parents (Eph. 6:1). But as a parent, obedience takes on a whole new light. I can now see why God loves obedience more than sacrifice (1 Sam. 15:22).

My firstborn is strong-willed, and I couldn't be prouder of her. No one loves Jesus more than Leslie. In her youth, though, we clashed. She didn't want to obey me unless she agreed with me. So, I routinely told her: "Obey first; then agree."

If we don't obey God until we agree with Him, it's going to be a tough life. We won't always understand or agree with His ways, but we can obey what we know. Imagine living with an obedience born not out of obligation but born from a passion to fulfill God's calling – to know and obey His will (Eph. 5:17, 6:6).

This truth hit home for me as a young door-to-door Bible salesman. In two summers, I knocked on 10,000 doors, talked with 4,200 people, and sold 700 Bibles. That's 14 doors and 6 no's for 1 sale. Although I was absolutely convinced that God called me to that job, I absolutely hated it. Each day, I asked myself: *Why in the world am I doing this?* And being 100% commission, I lived on rationed peanut butter sandwiches and mac 'n cheese. But then something happened that changed my life.

In desperation one morning, I begged God to show me what to do. So, I opened the Bible I was trying to sell, stuck my finger on a random page, and read Ephesians 4:1, which in that translation, read: "Be faithful to the vocation to which you were called." Wow! Those words pierced my soul and I thought: *Will I wholeheartedly obey God's calling to this job, or just comply?*

My sales didn't transform instantly, but my heart did. I still had questions about this calling, but my mission was transformed because I trusted that God's purpose was in it. It was the start of what I would tell Leslie 20 years later: Obey first; then agree.

Even Jesus had questions. As He was about to be crucified, Jesus prayed: "My Father, if it is possible, may this cup be taken from me. Yet not as I will, but as you will" (Matt. 26:39). He didn't want to be crucified, but He was willing to do so because He had already decided to obey His Father's will (Luke 9:51, 22:42).

True obedience is voluntary, not due to compulsion (1 Pet. 5:1-3). Even if it doesn't make sense, we must obey God with a wholeheartedness that is immediate, complete, joyful, and unconditional. It's a gift to give (not a burden to carry) when it's not shades of disobedience, per Ephesians 6:6-8.

Four Forms of Disobedience:

1. Delayed obedience

Delayed obedience is disobedience. We can't obey eventually; we must obey immediately from a servant heart. So too, God loves it when we obey because we want to, not because we're trying get something or win favor (Eph. 6:6).

2. Partial obedience

Partial obedience is disobedience. Complete obedience, though, flows from a whole heart (Eph. 6:7) and proves what's in our heart. Similarly, Jesus said that what defiles us is what comes out of us because it reflects what's in our heart (Mark 7:15).

3. Joyless obedience

Joyless obedience is disobedience. But joyful obedience does the
will of God because we serve God, not people (Eph. 6:7). Don't
be like the child who defiantly sat down and said, "I may be sitting
on the outside, but I'm standing on the inside." God expects us
to sit on the inside too because we're doing it as unto His heart.

4. Conditional obedience

Conditional obedience is disobedience. No condition warrants
anything less than wholehearted obedience, because our mission
is to honor God. Yes, He promises to reward us (Eph. 6:8) for
diligently seeking Him (Heb. 11:6), but diligence is living for our
God-given mission, not our own methods.

#4 Missional

Live for your mission, not your methods

*I pray that you, being rooted and established in love, may have
power, together with all the Lord's holy people, to grasp how wide
and long and high and deep is the love of Christ, and to know this
love that surpasses knowledge—that you may be filled to the
measure of all the fullness of God. – Eph. 3:17-19*

Is there anything – literally anything – you won't do to help your
family be faithful? Anything you won't stop? Won't start? Won't
change? Your family is your #1 mission, and God says this about
your family: "Whatever you do, work at it with all your heart, as
working for the Lord, not for human masters, since you know
that you will receive an inheritance from the Lord as a reward. It
is the Lord Christ you are serving" (Col. 3:23-24).

You may even know your God-given mission, but if you want
to know what you really treasure, look at your money and time.
Because money follows mission. And so does time. "Where your
treasure is, there your heart will be also" (Matt 6:21).

Does the mission you're living align with God's mission for you? You don't choose your mission; God does. You just choose if you'll discover it and live it. You can even do good things, but that's not being missional. Being missional is living according to God's mission for you.

Sometimes we're not missional because we don't understand God's methods. Noah didn't understand why God told him to build an ark, but Noah built it anyway and saved mankind. Abraham didn't understand why God told him to sacrifice his son, but he proceeded and God provided a sacrificial lamb instead. If you want God's blessings, trust His ways, not yours.

We're also not missional sometimes because we're married to our methods. Methods must adapt. For example, if you do the same things and complain about the same results, you're married to your method. And if you spend money and time the same ways you did years ago, you're married to your method.

Other times, we're not missional because our methods are misguided. I never want my message to be missed because my method is misguided. God never calls you to a method; He calls you to a mission. He never says, "Well done, good and faithful methods!"

We don't get to pick the parts of our mission that we like. For example, if we'll work harder on a task because we'll get paid more, we're not missional. We must give our all, no matter the task or the reward, because God blesses faithfulness to our mission, not fortune from our mission.

We also need to be careful with routines. Yes, routines are comfortable, but Dr. Nathan Jones taught me to always make new mistakes. That is, don't hold onto methods that don't work. But the flip side is to also ensure we're making new mistakes because we can't grow without them.

Is your life proof that God's will is "good, pleasing, and perfect" (Rom. 12:2)? Granted, you won't always be good, pleasing, and perfect, but your life can testify that God's will is. You can experience a metamorphosis explainable only by the fact that God does it, as you pursue the four goals of missional living from Ephesians 3:17-19.

Four Goals of Missional Living:

1. Grow rooted in God's love
Since our roots determine our fruits, we must be firmly "rooted and established" (Eph. 3:17) in the fertile love of God's good soil. Getting stuck in methods may be comfortable to us, but our family will experience the pain caused by the hardened, rocky, or thorny soil of our life (Mark 4).

2. Grasp the expanse of God's love
When we begin to "grasp how wide and long and high and deep is the love of Christ" (Eph. 3:18), we'll do anything to grab hold of what God loves, not cling to what we love. And once we grasp the expanse of His love, we'll live missionally for Him, which will help our family do the same.

3. Know God's surpassing love
To be missional is to "know this love that surpasses knowledge" (Eph. 3:19). And God's love is real. Nothing else even compares to knowing His surpassing love, surpassing worth (Phil. 3:8), surpassing power (Eph. 1:19), and surpassing peace (Phil. 4:7).

4. Be filled with God's love
Missional living allows us to "be filled to the measure of all the fullness of God" (Eph. 3: 19). Not a little filling, partial filling, or occasional filling. God wants us to be fully filled. And not filled to our fullness, but filled to all of *His* fullness – "good measure, pressed down, shaken together and running over (Luke 6:38a).

Please take a moment to score the healthy habits of T – Transforming mission on a scale of 1 (low) to 10 (high). And pick which of these four habits you want to grow first.

Transforming Mission		You	Home
<u>Success:</u>	*Know God's calling for you*	___	___
<u>Clarity:</u>	*Never live in the shadows of vague*	___	___
<u>Obedience:</u>	*Obey wholeheartedly, not compliantly*	___	___
<u>Missional:</u>	*Live for your mission, not your methods*	___	___
	Total	___	___
	/4 = Average	☐	☐

The Transforming mission habit I'll grow is: _____

A great first step to articulate a family mission is choosing your family's character qualities. That's the purpose of this next exercise taken from *Well Done, Mom and Dad!*

Exercise: "Secret Sauce"

Your A-to-Z family character qualities

Your family needs to know your "Secret Sauce" – the unique mix of character qualities that flavors everything you do. In this exercise, you choose 26 A-to-Z character qualities that you want to define your family. One quality for each letter of the alphabet.

I encourage families to have everyone pick their own A-to-Z character qualities, and then come together to choose them as a family. After Anna and I did this exercise separately, we met and changed 14 of my 26 A-to-Z qualities. Why? Because we wanted our list of character qualities to be how we, as a couple, would define our marriage and family. And, years later, it's still our roadmap for a spiritually vibrant family.

This exercise gets me emotional because it has impacted my family so significantly. For example, years after they picked their Secret Sauce, my son and his wife sent me a photo of them in a coffee shop, revising their A-to-Z character qualities because they were expecting their first baby. And then there is this little man: my grandson, Cade Bolder Medlin. Nicknamed "Cade the Bold," he's living proof of the power of character qualities . . . because his parents' "B" character quality is "Bold!"

There are so many ways to use your A-to-Z qualities. You can discuss them on family pizza nights, post them on a refrigerator, or discuss them at dinner. You might have family devotions to connect them to Scripture. I wrote 26 blogs to help our kids understand the qualities that Mom and I were trying to model for them. The possibilities are as endless as your imagination.

To make it easy for you, here are words to choose from. For each letter, circle one character quality that you want to define your family's character, or write in your own word.

A – Abide / Achieve / Affirm / Admirable / Adventure / Agreeable / Aligned / Ambitious / Amiable / Appreciative / Artistic / Ascend / Attentive /Authentic / Awaken / _____

B – Basic / Beacon / Beliefs / Believable / Belonging / Beloved / Best-practices / Biblical / Big-hearted / Blessing / Bold / Bonding / Boundless / Brave / Bright-eyed / _____

C – Captivate / Care / Challenging / Cheerful / Christ-like / Choices / Commit / Communicate / Compelling / Confident / Consistent / Contented / Courageous / Curious / _____

D – Daring / Decisive / Dedicated / Dependable / Determined / Devoted / Dignified / Diligent / Direct / Discerning / Discreet / Disciplined / Dreamer / Driven / _____

E – Eager / Earnest / Effective / Elevate / Embolden / Empathy / Empowering / Encourage / Endurance / Engage / Enhance / Enliven / Enthusiastic / Ethical / _____

F – Facilitate / Fair / Faithful / Family / Fearless / Fellowship / Fervent / Fidelity / Flexible / Flourish / Focus / Forgiving / Friend / Fulfill / Fun / Funny / Futuristic / _____

G – Generous / Gentle / Giver / Glow / Goal-oriented / Godly / Good-natured / Graceful / Gracious / Grateful / _____

H – Happy / Heart / Heaven-minded / Heighten / Heroic / Heritage / Holiness / Honest / Honorable / Hopeful / Hospitable / Humble / Humor / _____

I – Imaginative /Independent / Influence / Ingenious / Initiative / Inquisitive / Inspiring / Instiller / Integrity / Intelligent / Interdependent / Intriguing / Invigorate / _____

J – Jazzed / Jesus-follower / Jolly / Joyful / Judicious / Juggling / Justice / Justified / _____

K – Keen / Keystone / Kind / Kindred / Kingdom-minded / Kneeling / Known / _____

L – Laughter / Leader / Learner / Legacy / Likable / Limitless / Listener / Lively / Longsuffering / Loving / Loyal / _____

M – Magnetic / Magnify / Mature / Meaningful / Meditative / Memories / Memorable / Mentor / Merciful / Missional / Modest / More / Motivate / Musical / _____

N – Natural / Nevertheless / Noble / Nonconforming / Non-negotiable / Nonstop / Notable / Nurture / _____

O – Obedient / Observant / Open / Open-minded / Opportune / Optimistic / Orderly / Original / Outdo / Outstanding / Overcomer / Overflowing / Ownership / _____

P – Passionate / Patient / Peace / Persuasive / Pleasant / Polite / Positive / Practical / Prayer / Present / Principle / Productive / Propel / Protector / Provider / Purposeful / _____

Q – Qualified / Quality / Quest / Questioning / Quick-witted / Quiet / Quips / Quirky / Quizzical / Quotable / _____

R –Redeemed / Refreshing / Relational / Reliable / Repenting / Resolute / Resourceful / Respectful / Responsible / Restrained / Resurrected / Reverent / Role model / _____

S – Safe / Sanctified / Self-discipline / Sensitive / Sentimental / Servant / Servant-leader / Significance / Sincere / Spirit-filled / Strategic / Steward / Supportive / Surrender / _____

T – Tactful / Teachable / Teacher / Tenacious / Tender / Timeless / Thankful / Thoughtful / Thriving / Trainer / Transforming / Transparent/ Trustworthy / Truthful / _____

U – Unassuming / Unconventional / Undaunted / Understanding / Understated / Unentitled / Unique / Unintimidated / Unselfish / Unwavering / Upright / _____

V – Validating / Valor / Values / Versatile / Vibrant / Vigorous / Virtuous / Visionary / Vitalize / Vivid / Vulnerable / _____

W – Warrior / Well-done / Well-spoken / Wholesome / Willing / Winsome / Wise / Worry-free / Worshipful / _____

X – Xacting / Xcellence / Xceptional / Xciting / Xemplary / Xplore / Xpressive / Xtraordinary / Xuberant / _____

Y – Yearning / Yes-ma'am / Yoke-breaker / Yoked / Young-hearted / Yielding / Youthful / _____

Z – Zany / Zealous / Zero-excuses / Zest / Zip / Zoned-in / Zoo / Zoomed-in / _____

Here's an example of what your Secret Sauce might look like.

Alba Family "Secret Sauce"

Authentic *Beliefs* CHOICES

Devoted

Encourager *Family*

Generous Humor **Integrity**

Jesus-follower KIND

Legacy-maker

Memories **NEVERTHELESS**

Obedient

Purposeful RELATIONAL

Quality

SERVANT- Transforming

LEADER **UNENTITLED**

Visionary

WELL-DONE! *Xtraordinary*

Young-hearted **Zealous**

These character qualities can help you better understand your transforming mission so that you'll lay up heavenly treasures to lay down at the feet of Jesus – the next "H" big rock of a HEALTHY home.

Chapter 9

Big Rock #6:

H – Heavenly Treasures

Healthy treasures are a gift
for your heavenly Savior

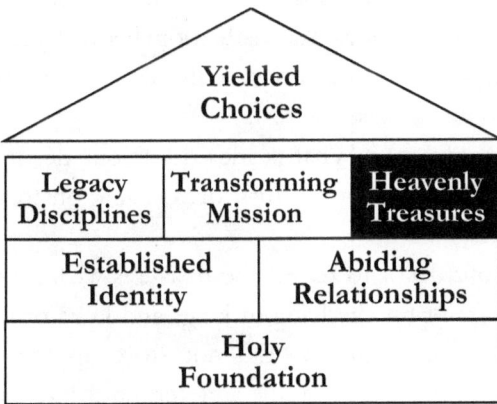

Yielded Choices		
Legacy Disciplines	Transforming Mission	**Heavenly Treasures**
Established Identity		Abiding Relationships
Holy Foundation		

Fill your house
with timeless *décor*

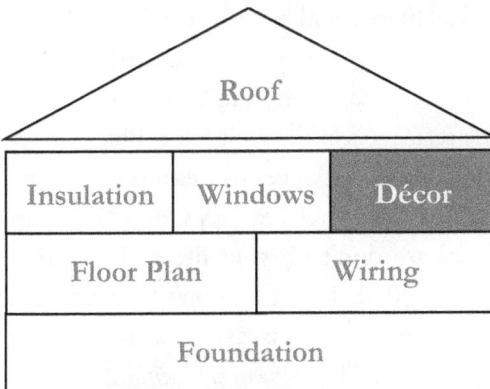

Roof		
Insulation	Windows	Décor
Floor Plan		Wiring
Foundation		

Now that your house is built, it's time to decorate it. As a boy, my room décor was sports posters and toy cars. As a young man, it was just stuff to fill space. But now I see décor differently.

Décor tells your story. I love seeing people's décor because I can tell more about you by what's in your house than by the house itself. Your house shows me the treasures you own, but your décor shows me what you treasure.

My posters and toy cars are long gone, exchanged for photos and purposeful paintings. But we didn't just add better things; we also replaced lesser things. We made room because you can't keep cramming more and more into your life. You have to decide what truly matters and release the rest.

What about you? What stories does your décor tell about you? Are you accumulating stuff, or focusing on treasures that truly matter?

I want our décor to reflect the treasures we'll lay at the feet of Jesus. Gifts fit for the King of kings and Lord or lords. Gifts that He says truly matter: "Do not store up for yourselves treasures on earth, where moths and vermin destroy, and where thieves break in and steal. But store up for yourselves treasures in heaven" (Matt. 6:19-20a).

Jesus said the kingdom of heaven is "like treasure hidden in a field. When a man found it, he hid it again, and then in his joy went and sold all he had and bought that field" (Matt. 13:44). The Apostle Paul instructed: "Set your minds on things above, not on earthly things" (Col. 3:2) in order to know Him, be found in Him, and attain the resurrection through Him (Phil. 3:8-11).

And even though God gives us treasures, they aren't ours. He owns them. We're just stewards of God's treasures for God's pleasure. So, please don't fill your life with "stuff." Fill it with fragrant treasures (Phil. 4:18) that don't burn up or fade away (1 Cor. 3:12). These are the only treasures worth accumulating – the second "H" of HEALTHY: *Heavenly treasures*.

One gift you can receive from Jesus is the crown of righteousness (2 Tim. 4:8) by living a holy life and looking forward to His return. Other examples are giving to the poor (Matt. 19:21), abandoning all to follow Him (Matt. 19:29), and lending to enemies (Luke 6:35). But another stored-up treasure that surely brings God joy is preparing your family to be biblical role models who are mature, generous, and resilient.

Role model	*Be the spittin' image of Jesus*
Maturity	*Grow with God's recipe of truth & love*
Generosity	*Overflow with lavish generosity*
Resilience	*Do your part & trust God to do His*

Living with a holy foundation, established identity, abiding relationships, legacy disciplines, and transforming mission prepares your family to fill their hearts with treasures that warm God's heart. Each big rock and each healthy habit can be a treasure you lay at His feet if you'll be a role model that your family wants to emulate.

#1 Role Model

Be the spittin' image of Jesus

Follow God's example, therefore, as dearly loved children – Eph. 5:1

The big question about newborns is: Who do they look like? Mom? Dad? A sibling? My 2-year-old grandson, Lewis, favors me, of course, even though some misguided people insist he looks like his other grandfather. It's okay, they can be wrong.

A bigger question, though, is: Who will Lewis act like when he's grown? His family, or a culture that rebuffs Jesus? If I had to pick anyone I want Lewis to act like, it's my dad. And, ironically, Lewis' dad (my son, Caleb) looks a lot like my dad, as shown in these photos taken 60 years apart.

Even better, though, is that Caleb's actions favor my dad and mom, who favor the Apostle Paul: "Follow my example, as I follow the example of Christ" (1 Cor. 11:1). My parents are too humble to say this about themselves, but I say it about them because they're role models of integrity.

To look like God, you don't have to be faultless, just faithful, like the four most influential ladies in my life. My wife is the finest person on the planet. My mom is loving and selfless. My sister, Sharon, is a champion of grace. And Anna's mom lovingly cared for her husband through 14 years of Alzheimer's. Each of these ladies is a role model for one reason: they favor Jesus Christ.

Your family's view of God is formed by watching you. Do you live with integrity? Do you protect your character? Do you live with the fruit of the Spirit? Even if you don't say, "Follow my example, as I follow Christ," that's what you hope they see in you.

So, mom, if you favor Jesus, your kids will likely rise up and bless you (Prov 31). And, dad, if your integrity is the spittin' image of Jesus, your kids will likely be the spittin' image of Jesus too.

Your treasures mold your family's treasures. And likely the best treasure you can give Jesus is a life of Christ-like integrity – integrity that is above reproach (1 Timothy 3, Titus 1). Christ-like integrity is more than just telling the truth. It's a heavenly treasure with three cornerstones: personal integrity, process integrity, and predictable integrity.

Three Cornerstones of Christ-like Integrity:

1. What you do (Personal integrity)

Satan first attacks your personal integrity – what you do. By killing your personal integrity, he kills your mission. He doesn't care about you; he just wants to destroy your impact. Like a politician, Satan digs up dirt to use against you. And like a boxer, he jabs until you let your guard down and then knocks you out.

The antidote? Personal integrity like Jesus. In the book of John, you can read about Jesus' divinity, character, and love.

2. How you do it (Process integrity)

If Satan can't disqualify your personal integrity, he'll attack your process integrity – how you do things. Because even if people agree with what you do, they'll get hung up on how you do it. If this happens to you, thwart the enemy's attacks by fixing the way you make choices, communicate those choices, and involve people in implementing those choices.

The antidote? Process integrity like Jesus. Luke's gospel account carefully examines *how* Jesus – the Son of Man – connects with us. As a human with emotions and pain, Jesus not only came to save people from all walks of life, He also showed us how to walk with others and connect them to the Father.

3. How consistently you do it (Predictable integrity)

If your personal and process integrity can't be crushed, the next target is your consistency – the predictability of your integrity. Can people count on you? The enemy loves to derail with minutia. Don't give him a foothold, no matter how small. Don't assume. Don't be inconsistent. Don't make promises you won't keep. Care enough to follow through. "It is better not to make a vow than to make one and not fulfill it" (Eccl. 5:5).

The antidote? Predictable integrity like Jesus, which is possible as we mature and become more like Him.

#2 Maturity

Grow with God's recipe of truth and love

Then we will no longer be infants, tossed back and forth by the waves, and blown here and there by every wind of teaching and by the cunning and craftiness of people in their deceitful scheming. Instead, speaking the truth in love, we will grow to become in every respect the mature body of him who is the head, that is, Christ. – Eph. 4:14-15

When Anna makes enchiladas, she follows a recipe. Still, she always spoons up a dab of sauce and asks me: "What do you think? What does it need?" She does this because even good recipes can need a little something different with each batch.

God's recipe of growth has two ingredients – truth and love. But we all need a slightly different mix of truth and love. For example, as noted earlier, I need extra respect and Anna needs extra love. It's the same with truth and love. I see life through a truth filter – love is great, but it's rudderless without godly truth. Anna, however, needs love before truth can stick. In reality, we're both right. But we're also both wrong if we don't balance God's truth with God's love.

In order to become mature in every respect like Christ and not be like "infants, tossed back and forth by the waves," we must speak the truth in love (Eph. 4:14-15). Otherwise, cunning and crafty people will deceive us and stunt our growth. And if we're not growing, we're dying.

"Truth in love" is a treasure we can give Jesus because it supercharges our spiritual growth and everyone we influence. As much as we need to remove our life weeds, we also need to overseed and fertilize our life and loved ones with truth and love. But before exploring a balance of truth and love, here's what it looks like when they're imbalanced:

Three Imbalances of Truth and Love:

1. Powerless truth   (Truth without love)

Truth without love is powerless and noisy (1 Cor 13:1). Truth is correct, accurate, and certain, but truth alone is disconnected, cold, and unrelatable. Without love, "I am nothing" and "I gain nothing" (1 Cor. 13:2,3). I can be 100% right, yet 0% potent because spiritual fruit doesn't grow without the root of truth and love. And God alone is truth (John 14:6) and love (1 John 4:8).

2. Misguided love   (Love without truth)

The opposite of powerless truth is misguided love – love without truth. It feels 100% right, yet it's 0% effective. Truthless love is a slippery slope to disaster. It promises what it can't deliver. Love is the greatest of all qualities (1 Cor. 13:13), but it isn't love unless it rejoices in the truth (1 Cor. 13:6). Truthless love is like "your truth" – it's not truth at all. You can build a home this way, but it will never be healthy.

3. Brokenness   (No truth, No love)

The saddest combo, though, is brokenness – no truth and no love. You don't see a better way, so you won't live a better way. Regardless of status, wealth, or power, we will all eventually feel broken, empty, and alone if we lack God's truth and love.

Thankfully, we don't have to live with these imbalances. God has an infinitely better plan for us, a way to experience the joy of balanced biblical truth and love: Maturity.

Proper balance of truth and love: Maturity

While Anna and I say we don't want our "perfect" little grandkids to grow up, we don't mean it. We just wish those early years could linger a bit. What we really want is for them to grow deep – to mature into the world-changers that God created them to be.

The world loves to quote John 8:32: "The truth will set you free." But it rejects the source of that truth, as explained in the prior verse: "If you (abide in) my teaching, you are really my disciples. Then you will know the truth, and the truth will set you free" (John 8:31-32). God's truth isn't powerless. It's powerful because it abides in its target – love. And God's love isn't misguided; it's missile-guided, so it always hits its target – truth.

Abiding in Jesus' truth and love is like what I think when I haven't seen my grandkids in a while: *How in the world did they grow so fast?* It happens because they've moved from milk to meat. Milk is great early on, but it's not enough for sustained growth.

So too, spiritual milk is great for infants, but it's not enough for adults. "Anyone who lives on milk, being still an infant, is not acquainted with the teaching about righteousness. But solid food is for the mature" (Heb. 5:13-14a).

Maturity is a heavenly treasure that brings joy, love, empathy, and perspective. It unleashes potential, fulfills purpose, and keeps us young-hearted. And, most importantly, maturity grows us deeper with Jesus so that we can become more like Him, especially with the next heavenly treasure: generosity.

#3 Generosity

Overflow with lavish generosity

In him we have redemption through his blood, the forgiveness of sins, in accordance with the riches of God's grace that he lavished on us. – Eph. 1:7-8a

Now to him who is able to do immeasurably more than all we ask or imagine, according to his power that is at work within us – Eph. 3:20

Although Anna wished I wasn't so "frugal" when we dated, we both wanted a marriage built on generosity. So, when I got an unexpected $300 bonus at my first job, we had a decision to make.

Anna wanted to buy a TV. And not just any TV. She wanted a *color TV!* Can you believe it? In 1984, that could have blown the whole $300. Instead, we gave three anonymous gifts of $100 to our three ministers, including our youth minister, Kent.

A few days later, Kent called and insisted we come over. He said he had prayed that morning for a $100 emergency and he couldn't believe that God answered his prayer. Yes, we later got a color TV, but that day we got something better – we saw that money is a tool to bless others, not a toy to bless us.

That's why before giving Ryan my blessing to marry Leslie, I asked him, "Ryan, I have one more question: Do you tithe?" He replied, "Yes, sir." And I said, "Awesome. I don't want my daughter to marry someone who robs God" (Mal. 3:8-10). I loved Ryan, but I had to know if he was obedient and generous.

While generosity is more than money, it can't exclude money. Over 2,000 Bible verses address money and possessions because of their incredible effects on spiritual health. The key is to live with less so that others can have more. And we can because we trust a lavish God to give us what we need (Eph. 1:8). Indeed, God loves to bless generosity (2 Cor. 9:6-8).

Generosity is the overflow of character. When character overflows, generosity overflows, as does contentment because we trust that His ways are higher than ours (Is. 55:9) and that He will do "immeasurably more than all we ask or imagine" (Eph. 3:20). "Give, and it will be given to you" (Luke 6:38a). "The generous will themselves be blessed" (Prov. 22:9). "It is well with the man who deals generously" (Ps. 112:5). Giving is a gift, not a transaction, and God blesses lavish generosity of all forms.

Are you lavish with time? Don't wait until you're not busy. Are you lavish with talents? Don't compare gifts with others; be thankful for *your* gifts. Are you lavish with money? God doesn't need your money, but He wants to bless others with it. Generosity may not be your spiritual gift, but you can give like it is.

In fact, the happiest people I know aren't the ones who get what they want; they're the ones who give away what they have. Here are four stages to build a heart of overflowing generosity.

Four Stages of Overflowing Generosity:

1. Empty everything you don't need

Overflowing starts with emptying yourself of whatever dilutes or clogs your life. What's that for you? Selfishness? Fame? Pride? Love of money? Whatever it is, get over it. There's not enough room in your heart for two masters (Matt. 6:24). The biggest impediments to generosity often aren't the big things; they're the little things you substitute for God's things.

2. Stop letting in everything you don't need

After emptying your life of any hindrances to generosity, don't let it get filled up right away. Let in what you need, not your "wants." Otherwise, you'll get caught up again with the sins that so easily entangle you (Heb. 12:1). Refuse to be like the Exodus Jews who wandered 40 years and kept returning to what they knew – the bondage that they had begged God to remove.

3. Keep being filled with what God wants

You can't just try to avoid the bad things. You have to keep being filled with the right things, starting with the best thing – the Holy Spirit. If you overflow with the Holy Spirit's filling, you'll overflow with the Holy Spirit's fruit (Gal. 5:22-23).

4. Open the floodgates of generosity

Finally, it's time to open the floodgates with the firstfruits of your time, talents, and treasures. Like a volcano, let your generosity spew (in a good way, of course) and watch God enrich others through it. And even if it just oozes sometimes, share how God has taught you to be generous, especially when tough times forced you to practice the next heavenly treasure: resilience.

#4 Resilience

Do your part and trust God to do His

Finally, be strong in the Lord and in his mighty power. – Eph. 6:10

When everything falls apart – when relationships sever, money disappears, and disease attacks – what happens? Sure, you'll go through the stages of grief like everyone else. But do you crack and crumble, or do you find a way to be resilient?

My sons are named Joshua and Caleb for one reason – I want them to be resilient and courageous like the two Exodus heroes who trusted God when the other ten spies didn't. Instead of just going along with the crowd, stand up and stand out by being stubborn with God's standard of faithfulness.

When Joshua took over for Moses, God told Joshua: "Be strong and courageous" (Josh. 1:6,7,9). So too, Ephesians ends with: "Finally, be strong in the Lord and in the power of his mighty power" (Eph. 6:10). And not just any ol' strength and power, but that which draws from two sources of God-honoring resilience: 1) being trustworthy and 2) trusting God.

First, are you trustworthy? Do people feel secure because they can trust you? Do you rise up, not give up? Persist, not quit? Stay the course, not sway with the tides? Trials will happen, but when they do, you can be strong and courageous because God is with you, interceding for you, guiding your steps, and protecting your path. Being trustworthy, though, isn't just determination. It takes both a want-to and a how-to. Both willing and able.

If you have a want-to but lack a how-to, you're a "can't." That is, you want to do what's needed, but you can't. No matter how great your attitude may be, you're incapable at this point, so you're not trustworthy. Willing, but unable.

Or maybe you're the opposite – a "won't." You have a how-to ability, but not a want-to attitude. You can, but won't. So, you're untrustworthy. Maybe, it's due to a lack of skill, but usually it's a lack of humility, urgency, or adaptability. Able, but unwilling.

Or maybe you're an "ain't," lacking both a want-to and a how-to. No matter how great an opportunity may be, you ain't gonna do it. It ain't happenin'. Unwilling and unable.

The point isn't to point fingers; it's to look in the mirror. Are you able (prepared) and willing (determined) to be faithful with opportunities? For while trust is earned over time, it can be lost in an instant. So, stay willing. Stay able. Stay resilient.

And second, do you trust God? No matter how hopeless things get, do you find hope in Him? A great example is Job: "The Lord gave and the Lord has taken away; may the name of the Lord be praised" (Job 1:21). I'm no Job, but when a boss tried to make me hide major financial problems, I had to quit. But I also had to trust God for my next paycheck (which, turns out, was better than the one I had). Only God!

If Job doesn't win the gold medal for resilience, Paul does: "I press on toward the goal to win the prize for which God has called me heavenward in Christ Jesus" (Phil. 3:14). And He "who began a good work in you will carry it on to completion until the day of Christ Jesus" (Phil. 1:6). Job and Paul could live this way because they were trustworthy and trusting God.

Will you get a crown of resilience? Are you fighting the good fight, finishing your course, and keeping the faith (2 Tim. 4:7-8)? Are you fulfilling your ministry and persevering in trials (Acts 20:24, James 1:12)? That's godly resilience – keep doing your part and trusting God to do His. And here are its three "rules."

Three Rules of Godly Resilience:

1. **You commit; God directs your plans**

    "Commit to the Lord whatever you do, and He will establish your plans" (Prov. 16:3)

Strategies and tactics are good, but that's not where resilience starts. It starts where the Macedonian church started. Despite extreme poverty, the Macedonians gave "beyond their ability" because they first gave themselves to God (2 Cor. 8:3-5).

Thus, we first commit our works to God and trust Him to direct our plans. Yes, we plan, but we don't plan first. We first commit to God, which enables us to do the second rule of resilience: make plans according to His will.

2. You plan; God directs your steps

"In their hearts humans plan their course, but God establishes their steps" (Prov. 16:9)

After committing your works, make your plans. No matter how good or bad your plans may be, though, God ultimately directs your steps. He doesn't tell you to not plan. He just wants you to let Him direct your steps – to willingly let Him be in charge and redirect the steps you had planned.

He also does something else we don't always grasp – God nudges our rudder without steering our ship. We hold the wheel while He's under the surface, directing where we go. The amount of His nudging depends on what we need. Sometimes gentle; sometimes not. Either way, He prepares us for the final rule of resilience: victory comes from God.

3. You prepare; God brings the victory

"The horse is made ready for the day of battle, but victory rests with the Lord" (Prov. 21:31)

After committing and planning, it's time to prepare and execute. This isn't tentative or wishful action. It's confidence in knowing who brings the victory – God. I must trust God to decide what is best. But if God's answer isn't what I hoped for, there's still victory.

Victory isn't getting what you want; it's preparing for what God wants. You can't force victory, so you can't claim it. But you can give credit where it's due. And since God alone brings the victory, all victories and credit are His.

Your part	God's part
Commit ➡	Directs your plans
Plan ➡	Directs your steps
Prepare ➡	Brings your victory

God expects us to do our part – commit, plan, and prepare. And He expects us to trust Him with His part – direct our plans, direct our steps, and bring victory. Our job is to be resilient spiritual gardeners who are trustworthy to prepare for a harvest and trust that a harvest will come from Him, our Rainmaker.

Please take a moment to score these four healthy habits of H – Heavenly treasures for you and your home. And select one of these four healthy habits that you'll grow for your family.

Heavenly Treasures

		You	Home
Role model:	*Be the spittin' image of Jesus*	___	___
Maturity:	*Grow with God's recipe of truth & love*	___	___
Generosity:	*Overflow with lavish generosity*	___	___
Resilience:	*Do your part & trust God to do His*	___	___
	Total	___	___
	/4 = Average	☐	☐

The Heavenly treasures habit I'll grow is: _____

The next exercise is a simple way to help your family celebrate the heavenly treasures that you will lay at Jesus' feet.

Exercise: "Treasured Memories"

The eternal difference you make

Before attending the funeral of a friend, Anna texted his widow about how he would dress up as "Superkid" to lead preschool worship. Every Sunday, the kids would scream, "Su-per-kid! Su-per-kid!" It was awesome. Only God knows how much Superkid prepared those little kids to love Jesus.

At the funeral, the family asked us all to take a 3x5 card and write how this friend had impacted our lives, especially spiritually. Then they gathered the cards to read at their first Thanksgiving without him. Turns out, Anna's text about Superkid helped the family celebrate his heavenly treasures. And that's what this exercise does, without waiting for a funeral to start.

Here's how it works: At the top of a 3x5 card, write the date on the left and their name on the right. Then write a memory of how they impacted you for eternity and sign it at the bottom. Whether it's a big thing or a little breadcrumb of faithfulness, share how they've blessed you.

Date	**Their name**
You are such a blessing to me because of how you're always _____	
Your signature	

And on the back of the card, write a funny memory about them or a memorable time with them. For example, if I wrote a "treasured memories" card for my son Caleb, I'd write on the front that I admire his uncompromising character and his passion for being a great husband and dad. And on the back, I'd tell his famous jaguar story (inside joke).

> One of my favorite stories about you was the time you _____
>
>

While this is a fun exercise to do anytime, it can also be an annual tradition, like birthdays or wedding anniversaries. It can be funny or serious. Recent or old history. Private or well-known. Just make it personal.

If you'll keep writing treasured memories cards, your family will keep re-reading them. They'll look forward to their next birthday or anniversary, knowing another card awaits with another story and encouraging word.

These cards, though, aren't just 3x5's to store in a closet. They're treasures to store in your heart – reminders that personal investments draw interest that compounds for eternity, as long as you live the last big rock of spiritual health: "Y" – Yielded choices.

Chapter 10

Big Rock #7:

Y – Yielded Choices

Healthy choices yield
to God's will

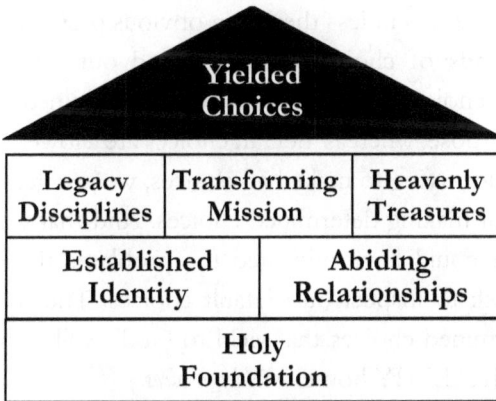

Yielded Choices		
Legacy Disciplines	Transforming Mission	Heavenly Treasures
Established Identity		Abiding Relationships
Holy Foundation		

Inspect your house
for a compromised *roof*

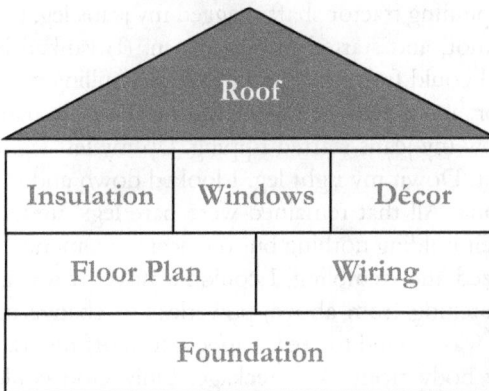

Roof		
Insulation	Windows	Décor
Floor Plan		Wiring
Foundation		

Congratulations! Your house is built and you're ready to move in, except for one thing. Have you inspected the roof? A roof is vital, as it covers and protects against seasonal extremes and outside elements that cause leaks due to buckling and curling. You'll likely inspect your roof when buying a house, but how often do you inspect it later for compromises? The answer, by default, is rarely unless you determine there's an obvious problem.

We assume our roof is okay. And so it is with our life choices – our spiritual roof – that covers everything in our lives. We rarely inspect our choices unless there's an obvious problem.

Two kinds of choices define us and our family's future: determined choices and default choices. Determined choices are made on purpose; whereas, default choices are allowed to happen.

We're not trying to make bad choices; we just get the default result of not making determined choices. And that's maddening because we could have mitigated the problems if we had just stepped back to inspect our default choices. The solution? To make determined choices that yield to God's will – the "Y" big rock of a HEALTHY home: *Yielded choices.*

As noted in *Well Done, Mom & Dad!,* this truth was seared into my soul as a teenage farm hand while mindlessly stacking hay bales on a conveyor, when suddenly. . .

> A spinning tractor shaft snagged my jeans leg, twisted it into a knot, and started pulling me in. (I) yanked back as hard as I could from the tractor that was pulling me toward death or a crippled, mangled future. Then it happened. Somehow my jeans started ripping. Up my left leg. Across my waist. Down my right leg. I looked down and my jeans were gone. All that remained were bare legs, undershorts, and a belt holding nothing but tiny jeans fragments.
>
> Dazed and trembling, I couldn't move. It was as if I'd been watching from above, powerless to change my fate. No one was around to see it happen, turn off the tractor, or pull my body from the wreckage. Only God could have miraculously ripped away those jeans. (And although I)

never meant to dangle my jeans over a tractor shaft. It just happened. So too, we don't intentionally dangle our kids over danger. Still, it happens, causing (us) to feel stripped down to (our) emotional nakedness, asking, "How in the world did my kids get snagged by my default choices?"

A near-tragic incident like that can shake us to our core. But unless we develop a habit of determined yielded choices, we get the default results of dangling our family over danger.

Yielded choices don't happen because we allow them to happen. They happen when we yield to God's will and God's way.

When accepting Jesus as our Savior, we make the ultimate determined choice – to turn away from sin and embrace Jesus. As time passes, though, we stop looking for the little compromises that cause big problems. Instead of yielding to God's commands or slowing down to look for danger, we disregard the warning signs, press on the gas, and hope we don't crash.

Spiritual health, though, doesn't just hope you won't crash. It keeps you from crashing. Like an uncompromised spiritual roof, here are four determined choices to stay healthy and not crash: Choose God's armor; Pre-choose boundaries of purity; Un-choose the old you; and Re-choose the Spirit's filling.

Choose	*Choose the perfect outfit: God's armor*
Pre-choose	*Pre-choose boundaries of purity*
Un-choose	*Un-choose the old you for a new you*
Re-choose	*Re-choose the filling that fuels & fulfills*

Yielded choices protect you from buckling due to ongoing sins. They cover you from little compromises that endanger your family. And they position everyone you influence to withstand life's seasonal extremes. Yielded choices start, though, with the fundamental daily choice of wearing the full armor of God.

#1 Choose

Choose the perfect outfit: God's armor

Put on the full armor of God, so that when the day of evil comes, you may be able to stand your ground, and after you have done everything, to stand. Stand firm then, with the belt of truth buckled around your waist, with the breastplate of righteousness in place, and with your feet fitted with the readiness that comes from the gospel of peace. In addition to all this, take up the shield of faith, with which you can extinguish all the flaming arrows of the evil one. Take the helmet of salvation and the sword of the Spirit, which is the word of God. – Eph. 6:13-17

"Hmmm. What should I wear?" Every morning, my wife ponders this question, intently seeking the perfect outfit. Today's outfit differs from yesterday, yet she somehow chooses the perfect outfit for each day. I, on the other hand, decide in 10 seconds because I don't have outfits. Just clothes. I grab whatever is there, unless Anna says, "You're not wearing THAT, are you?"

What you wear shows what you're preparing for. If you're wearing jogging clothes, you're ready to jog. For cold weather, it's a coat. And when you're preparing for the enemy's flaming arrows, you put on God's armor – His belt of truth, breastplate of righteousness, shoes of the gospel of peace, shield of faith, helmet of salvation, and sword of the Spirit (Eph. 6:13-17).

By default, we're unprepared for spiritual attacks because we're not wearing God's armor. The question isn't if we'll face spiritual warfare; it's if we're prepared when it comes.

So, where does Satan attack? It's where you're unprotected. Didn't put on His belt of truth today? You'll likely be tempted to believe a lie. Didn't grab His breastplate of righteousness? Get ready for a "little" sin with big consequences.

We must wear each piece of God's armor because each piece is crucial. And each piece fits each occasion. Here are five protections we get by making the determined choice to put on God's armor and keep it on.

Five Protections of God's Armor:

1. Protects your character
Winning spiritual warfare starts with protecting your character, which starts with emulating Jesus' character. God's armor shields you from the enemy's flaming arrows. So, if you're not wearing it, Satan's arrows can easily puncture your character.

2. Protects your caring
Caring with your own strength might seem fine, but it doesn't work. Healthy homes care enough to clothe themselves with God's armor. It's a spiritual version of how my mom would bundle me up to play in Iowa winters. Protecting your family with God's armor shows how much you care for them.

3. Protects your consistency
My dad is my hero in part because he's so consistent. As a kid, I didn't get why he'd turn off the TV when bad language came on. I didn't get why we attended church so much. I didn't get why we prayed before every meal. But I get it now. It was the result of consistently putting on God's armor.

4. Protects your courage
When my young kids got scared, they hid behind me because they felt safe as long as they were with me. But now, no matter how scary life may get, their fears can be replaced with courage by standing fully armed behind their Heavenly Father.

5. Protects against complacency
Wolves often come in sheep's clothing. But our worst enemy can be familiarity, which leads to complacency – a slow killer. The solution is putting on God's armor and keeping it on. Nothing is

better than God's armor to protect your family from a society that opens the gate for the enemy to attack.

God's armor is also like a spiritual sunscreen that blocks out Satan's harmful effects. You'll get burned if it's not applied consistently and if it doesn't cover all of you. And as we'll see next, if you don't also pre-choose boundaries of purity, you negate the power of God's armor.

#2 Pre-choose

Pre-choose boundaries of purity

There must not be even a hint of sexual immorality, or of any kind of impurity, or of greed, because these are improper for God's holy people. – Eph. 5:3

Have nothing to do with the fruitless deeds of darkness, but rather expose them. It is shameful even to mention what the disobedient do in secret. – Eph. 5:11-12

I was once nearly fired because I was accused of being "godlike, arrogant, and rude." Then, I found $7 million of problems that my accusers had hidden. Although falsely accused, I learned a valuable lesson: Don't do anything that even hints at wrongdoing. Don't dangle or even get close to lines we shouldn't cross.

When King David saw a bathing woman, his gaze led to adultery, murder, and pain for a whole nation. It's like what Dr. Jimmy Draper says, "Sin always hurts innocent people." If only David had pre-chosen boundaries of purity. That's proactive purity – choosing your response before you're tempted.

Proactive purity takes years to build, but it can be lost in a moment. And while all impurity is repulsive to God (Ps. 5:5), sexual impurity has greater consequences. It's a sin against your own body (1 Cor. 6:18). "Have nothing to do with the fruitless deeds of darkness" (Eph. 5:11). "It is shameful even to mention what the disobedient do in secret" (Eph. 5:12).

What happens when we sneak a peek? We get burned. I'll never forget the day I opened my gas grill and a grease fire exploded. The burgers weren't the only thing that got burned. My eyebrows were singed off too. While I learned a lesson about grilling, I was also reminded that we'll get burned if we're close to sin. Unlike eyebrows that easily regrow, though, purity is not easily restored. Its consequences leave lasting scars after ravaging the family and legacy we've worked so hard to build.

We're tempted because we drop our guard, ignore blind spots, or get hardened. Either way, we lose because we're trying to put new wine into old wineskins that can't expand to handle the fermenting dangers of temptation.

Pre-choosing boundaries is also needed because anyone can be accused. The question is: Will people believe you? A co-worker used to taunt me for never being alone with female staff. But then his playful bantering with a female co-worker nearly got him fired. He dangled over the edge and nearly got snagged.

We need to instead be like Buckingham Palace soldiers, standing guard over these three principles of proactive purity:

Three Principles of Proactive Purity:

1. Decide before you're tempted
When teenager Josh would go hang out with friends, his older sister would say, "Have fun. Be pure!" While funny, she was making a point: pre-choose purity. Wearing a purity ring or wedding ring is great, but it won't stop sin after it starts. We must choose *before* temptation happens. And if we think we're stronger than King David, we're not. If the man after God's heart could fall into impurity, what makes us think we can't?

2. **Run away when you're tempted**

What do you do when you're tempted? My solution at work was to sprint down the hall. My team laughed at my silly approach to temptation, but it was a reminder to protect my family and me from the pain of immorality, greed, and impurity (Eph. 5:3). Even a *hint* of impurity turns into a *hunt* for impurity.

3. **Repent after you're tempted**

But what do you do after you're tempted? First, repent by asking for God's forgiveness because "each person is tempted when they are dragged away by their own evil desire" (James 1:14). Next, repent by turning away from sin and running to God. And last, repent by thanking Him for restoration and the strength to run! "God is faithful; he will not let you be tempted beyond what you can bear. But when you are tempted, he will also provide a way out so that you can endure it" (1 Cor. 10:13).

Pre-choosing your response simplifies life. Temptations still occur, but if you're proactively pure, you're only reinforcing what you've already decided, not making difficult choices when you can't think straight. And with a pure life, you can live a new life by un-choosing your old nature for a new nature.

#3 Un-choose

Un-choose the old you for a new you

Put off your old self, which is being corrupted by its deceitful desires; to be made new in the attitude of your minds; and to put on the new self, created to be like God in true righteousness and holiness. – Eph. 4:22b-24

Back in the day, it was a contest of who'd be the most excited when I got home – my kids or our dog, Abbie. But over time, only Abbie stayed excited to see me. While I wish my kids had kept Abbie's fervor, I'm glad they didn't copy one of Abbie's other habits – eating her vomit. Yep, as gross as it was to see our dog do that, it must be far worse for God to see us revert to our disgusting habits. "As a dog returns to its vomit, so fools repeat their folly" (Prov. 26:11).

Paul's solution is to "put off your old self, which is being corrupted by its deceitful desires" (Eph. 4:22b). Thankfully, as a Christian, you don't have to let your old self define you. In Christ, you can un-choose the old you and "be made new in the attitudes of your mind" (Eph. 4:23) because you're "created to be like God in true righteousness and holiness" (Eph. 4:24).

To get where you need to be, you need to un-choose what got you here. Let God give you a new path and attitude. You can't un-do your old corrupt, deceitful desires on your own because only God can do that for you. But you can "put them off" – forcefully, deliberately shed your former ways – by un-choosing your old nature for a new nature in Christ.

To live according to your new nature, you can't "indulge in every kind of impurity," "let any unwholesome talk come out of your mouths," or "give the devil a foothold" (Eph. 4:19, 29, 27). These relics of the old you can't co-exist with the new you in Christ because God won't look at or tolerate sin (Hab. 1:13). But before we review how to un-choose our past, let's consider what un-choosing is not.

First, un-choosing is not just trying harder. God condemns not trying (Matt. 25:26-30), but trying harder alone is a recipe for failure. Second, it's not just being positive. While positivity is powerful, it won't keep us from returning to our spiritual vomit. Third, it's not just claiming victory. We pray for God's victory in His name, but name-it-claim-it is a lie from the pit of hell. And fourth, un-choosing is not just hoping for better. Hope is great. But if hope doesn't result in real life, it's not real hope. Hope learns from the past yet yearns for a fresh future.

Un-choosing burns the ships of the old you to discover a new you in God's "true righteousness and holiness" (Eph. 4:24). But when you revert sometimes (we all do), don't stay there. Here's a three-step change in Ephesians 4:22-24 to help you un-choose your past and live victoriously as a new you in Christ.

Three Changes for a New You:

1. Spiritual insanity: Do the same things in the same ways and hope for better.

Recovery starts with admitting a problem exists. So too, un-choosing your past starts with admitting you've been doing the same things in the same ways and hoping for better. That's spiritual insanity. Transformation requires change. You must "put off your old self, which is being corrupted by its deceitful desires" (Eph. 4:22) to get to the second step of change.

2. Spiritual absurdity: Do different things in different ways and hope for better.

Jesus told Nicodemus that he must be born again (John 3:3). And that requires big change. But change for change's sake – doing different things in different ways and hoping for better – is spiritual absurdity. Instead of just a tweaked you, make room for a transformed you: "made new in the attitude of your minds" (Eph. 4:23). Then you're ready for the final step of change.

3. Spiritual certainty: Do the right things in right ways and trust God for better.

The final step of change is to put on a new self – do the right things in right ways and trust God for better. That's spiritual certainty. You become "like God in true righteousness and holiness" (Eph. 4:24). That's not a possibility or a probability. That's a certainty because He promised it and you can trust Him, just like you can trust that He offers eternal life (1 John 5:13), that

He answers your prayers (1 John 5:14-15), and that He supplies all your needs according to His riches (Phil. 4:19). And you can trust Him to bless you: "How much more will your Father in heaven give good gifts to those who ask him!" (Matt. 7:11).

By living the new nature God intends for you, you're ready for the final yielded choice that fuels your soul and fulfills God's will: letting the Holy Spirit fill you.

#4 Re-choose

Re-choose the filling that fuels and fulfills

Do not get drunk on wine, which leads to debauchery. Instead, be filled with the Spirit. – Eph. 5:18

Christianity is built on irony. Die to you and live for Christ. In your weakness, He is made strong. The first shall be last and the last, first. Be free by being Christ's slave. A perfect God died for imperfect people. And empty yourself to be filled by the Spirit.

But how is that possible? It's possible through irony – by proactively being passive. On the surface, that doesn't make sense. But in the Spirit, it's a command to intentionally let Him take control (Eph. 5:18). The Greek word for "be filled" in this context is the ultimate irony: to be dominated or controlled. That is, to yield our will to His will and rely on Him to dominate us.

We're dominated by whatever dominates us (2 Pet. 2:19), so God wants us to be dominated by the Holy Spirit. He fires us up and fuels our passion in order to fulfill His will and delight His heart. His filling comforts, guides, instructs, convicts, encourages, and empowers us to walk according to His will.

"Be filled" is also an ongoing action – what you have done, are doing, and will keep doing. It's a lifestyle of re-choosing His filling, no matter how ironic or unnatural it may seem.

A close cousin of irony is contrast-and-comparison, which Ephesians 5:18 uses with drunkenness and the Spirit's filling. By contrast, drunkenness leads to debauchery, but the Spirit's filling leads to the fruit of the Spirit. The former pushes you away from intimacy with God; the latter pulls you into His presence.

But there also is a comparison with drunkenness and the Spirit's filling. In both, you release control, allowing something to control the choices that control you. Re-choosing the Spirit's filling drives out what keeps you from God and draws in what keeps you close to Him.

This one choice – what you allow to control you – determines your destination. Like a tiny rudder that controls a huge ship (James 3:4), your spiritual destination is determined by what you keep re-choosing. Every time you re-choose His filling, it's easier to make another great determined choice. And every time you allow something else to replace the Spirit, you're more likely to make another lousy default choice.

Spiritual protection is a dual choice – don't let "tiny" sins metastasize, and let the Spirit constantly fill us. The key to doing both is to keep yielding to Him. It starts by choosing His protective armor, pre-choosing His purity, and un-choosing our old nature for a new nature in Him. But we also need to keep re-choosing these four renewals of spiritual health.

Four Renewals of Spiritual Health:

1. Refill

Some people see their spiritual glass as half full or half empty. But what God sees is whether or not you're refilling your spiritual glass. If you want more of God's filling, ask and believe that He will. Please don't treat your spiritual life like a gas tank that gets dangerously low. Running on empty is no way to live the Christian life. Keep on getting refilled with the Spirit.

2. Refresh

The Spirit's filling isn't just for your heart; it's also for your mind. "(Keep on being) transformed by the renewing of your mind" (Rom. 12:2a). The only way to stay fresh is to stay full, which requires constant refreshing. Otherwise, your heart and mind will turn from being a flowing, refreshing Jordan River into a lifeless Dead Sea that receives but never gives.

3. Re-position

Spiritual health also isn't a satellite that you point once in the right direction. It's a moving target. For example, I had a one-size-fits-all approach as a parent, but I'm learning to re-position myself to meet each child's needs. And that takes spiritual stretching, which is a great way to keep yourself spiritually limber.

4. Repeat

Like spiritual shampoo, learn to lather, rinse, and repeat. Lather up in God's presence, rinse out sin, and repeat. Over and over. Day after day. Constantly repeat this simple plan to fuel and fulfill your calling. It's a formula to not only get spiritually clean, but also stay clean.

More than a plan to follow, your family needs you to follow God's plan. They need to see you re-choosing the Spirit's filling and they need you to keep re-teaching them how. For example, Leslie still talks about how, as a little girl, she memorized Scripture while washing dishes with Mom. That repetition prepared Leslie to be great mom years later. She wasn't just memorizing Scripture; she was learning how to stay fueled and fulfilled.

Please take a moment to score these four healthy habits of Y – Yielded choices for you and your home. Also, please pick one of the Yielded choices habits that you'd like most to grow.

Yielded Choices		You	Home
Choose:	*Choose the perfect outfit: God's armor*	___	___
Pre-choose:	*Pre-choose boundaries of purity*	___	___
Un-choose:	*Un-choose the old you for a new you*	___	___
Re-choose:	*Re-choose the filling that fuels & fulfills*	___	___
	Total	___	___
	/4 = Average	☐	☐

The Yielded choices habit I'll grow is: _____

Anyone can talk about great choices. The question is: Will you just talk about them, or will you act? One of my favorite quotes on action came from my son after one of our family exercises: "It's useful if refined over several years of growth and change. But it shouldn't stop there. It should be composed of goals that propel me to action."

Here's an exercise called "3-2-1 Impacts" to help you and your family take action and impact others, using more 3x5 cards.

Exercise: "3-2-1 Impacts"

Intentionally impact others

A friend once told me, "When you're a learner, everyone is a teacher." No matter the circumstance or problem, we can learn. No matter if the "teacher" is a good example or a bad example, we can learn. And we must learn because our loved ones depend on us to make yielded choices that impact eternity.

Who has impacted you? A grandparent or parent? A spouse? Coach? Friend? Minister? The older I get, the more I want to "impact it forward" – impact people who, in turn, will impact others for eternity. Two of the many people who have impacted me are Scotty Sanders and Joe Croce.

As explained in his book *Life on a 3x5: A Framework for Daily Success*, Scotty creates daily success plans on 3x5 cards. It's a simple, powerful way to choose a few key things each day that make the biggest impact.

And Joe Croce, founder of CiCi's Pizza, showed us how to wow 100 million guests annually with excellence, simplicity, and intentionality. For example, in our store managers' shirt pockets was a 3x5 card with the critical few priorities of great restaurants. Our managers knew they'd be successful if they excelled in that 3x5 card's list of priorities.

Scotty and Joe used 3x5 cards to simplify the complex, making it easy to make great choices. So, I borrowed from them to create this simple tool, "3-2-1 Impacts":

3 people … 2 impacts … 1 action

Each week, on a 3x5 card, write the names of 3 people in which you want to invest. Then write 2 impacts you want to make in each of those people and 1 action you'll take this week to impact them. That's it. But if you'll do this each week for a month, imagine the effect. And if you'll keep doing this for a year, imagine how you could impact their eternity.

Your "3 people" will surely change as needs change, as God prompts you, or as birthdays and anniversaries approach. And instead of a person, your "3 people" might be groups like your kids, church small group, neighbors, or co-workers. Also, you'll likely change the impacts you want to make over time. In fact, your impacts should change as needs and relationships change.

While this exercise lists your impacts and actions, the focus isn't on you. It's on the needs of the people God wants you to impact.

In order to keep your desired impacts top of mind, you might put your 3-2-1 Impacts lists in a wallet, purse, or office. Or maybe you'll post them on a mirror, car dashboard, or refrigerator.

However you do it, though, just make sure they stay fresh and visible. Here's how your weekly 3x5 cards might look:

__3 People__	__2 Impacts__	__1 Action__
Person/Group 1	_____	_____
	_____	
Person/Group 2	_____	_____
	_____	
Person/Group 3	_____	_____
	_____	

As you apply the 7 Big Rocks and 28 healthy habits of HEALTHY in your life and home, you won't always know exactly what to do or how they'll take root. But you can be certain that they won't "return void" (Is. 55:11). God will use them to keep you and your family spiritually healthy if, according to the next chapter's principles, you'll live a spiritually healthy lifestyle.

Chapter 11

Live a Spiritually Healthy Lifestyle

Three times, I've lost 30+ pounds, which means I've gained 30+ pounds three times. My weight is a roller coaster, up and down, but rarely the same. If I'm not intentionally eating healthy, my willpower loses out to my love of pizza, pasta, and chips. The problem often isn't getting fit; it's staying fit.

Fluctuating weight is the result of not fully dedicating myself – not setting my heart – to physical health. And even though I tend to lose perspective about my weight, it's obvious to you because you can see the results of my habits.

It's a physical version of the spiritual roller coaster found in 2 Chronicles 12:14: "He did evil because he did not set his heart on seeking the Lord." It's not that this man tried to dedicate himself to the wrong things; he just wasn't dedicated to the right things, which hurt his family and his nation.

Spiritual health is much the same. We're either getting closer to God or further from him, but rarely staying the same. And if we don't fully dedicate ourselves to God, it's obvious to others, especially the people it harms the most – our family. The way to get off that spiritual roller coaster is to set our hearts on getting spiritually healthy and staying there.

That requires willpower, but willpower isn't enough. You also need to practice the three keys to living a spiritually healthy lifestyle – a healthy spiritual metabolism, preventive spiritual care, and an intimate relationship with Jesus.

Spiritual metabolism
Preventive spiritual care
Relationship with Jesus

Spiritual metabolism

Turn dieting into a healthy spiritual metabolism

If your metabolism is messed up, so are you. I first saw this as a young door-to-door salesman. I worked 13+ hours a day for months without stopping to buy food. I saved enough money to finish college, but it messed up my metabolism.

A few years later, I was so desperate to lose weight, for months I had no breakfast, a diet soda for lunch, and a small dinner. It worked at first. I lost 45 pounds. But I became even more susceptible to a roller coaster of weight gain.

I've tried all kinds of diets. Some worked for a while, but I soon regressed, more frustrated than when I started because I thought I just needed to try harder. Finally, Anna and I took a healthy lifestyles class to learn a lifestyle of healthy metabolism.

So too with spiritual health. It's not spiritual dieting. Not fads. Not techniques. It's a lifestyle with a healthy spiritual metabolism that consumes biblical truth and exercises that truth. The key to replacing your spiritual love handles with a six pack of spiritual strength is practicing these five metabolism-building habits.

1. Drink plenty of spiritual water

Physical health starts with drinking 100 ounces of water per day for men and 90 ounces for women. Not fancy energy drinks, coffees, sodas, or supplements. Just regular ol' water, an essential element of life and the most abundant molecule on Earth.

Spiritual health also requires adequate hydration with large amounts of the most basic elements of spiritual water – Bible study and prayer. Yes, it's hard to find time for adequate Bible study and prayer, but the consequences of spiritual dehydration are tragic.

2. Consume balanced spiritual meals

By planning meals in advance, we make better food decisions. So too, pre-planning our spiritual nutrition helps us make healthier spiritual decisions and reduces our spiritual aches and pains.

Prior chapters provided a framework of healthy spiritual meals that strengthens our spiritual immunity and metabolism, but we have to consume them. Don't starve yourself spiritually. Don't eat spiritual junk food. Consume balanced spiritual meals, including in-person worship and fellowship. And don't forget repentance. When you fall off the wagon (we all do sometimes), you need to receive God's forgiveness and forgive yourself.

3. Strengthen your spiritual core

Physical health is improved by what you lose (weight) and what you gain (strength). When my back hurts, the fix is almost always a stronger core – the interconnected muscles of our mid-section that gives stability, balance, and improved function.

Likewise, you need to strengthen your spiritual core with fasting, Bible memorization, and journaling. That improves your metabolism, helps you function better, and replaces your spiritual flab with stamina and balance. But if you neglect your spiritual core, you'll likely experience spiritual inflexibility and atrophy.

4. Exercise your spiritual gifts

My mother-in-law is older than most of her friends, yet she looks younger. What's her secret? Regular exercise. She doesn't always want to attend her exercise class, but she has for decades.

You won't always feel like spiritually exercising either, but you need to keep stretching yourself by serving, giving, mentoring, and witnessing. Many spiritual exercises are common to all of us, but you also need to exercise your unique spiritual gifts like an extra measure of serving, giving, encouraging, teaching, leading, granting mercy, or prophesying (Rom. 12:6-8).

5. Rest for spiritual well-being

A healthy spiritual metabolism doesn't happen by default or osmosis. It requires ongoing, determined action. But if the pendulum swings too far the other way, you'll miss the last key to having a six-pack of spiritual strength – rest.

You can't serve God well unless you rest well. Rest isn't just a good idea. It's the fourth commandment (Ex. 20:8). Great rest enables great faithfulness. And while you may rest in unique ways, I find that worship music and serving others will refresh my soul more than extra sleep. What refreshes you?

After you've built a healthy metabolism with spiritual water, balanced spiritual meals, a strong spiritual core, spiritual exercise, and spiritual rest, you're ready for the second key to a healthy lifestyle – preventive spiritual care.

Preventive spiritual care

Turn emergency care into preventive spiritual care

Like the hero in the movie *Taken*, my friend Gary Phillips has a very particular set of skills acquired over a long career. His best skill is something we all need – turning chaos into order. Gary and I worked well together, in part, because I complement him with a different skill – preventing chaos. Gary gets you out of emergencies and people like me help you not live there.

Emergencies are part of life, but why endure them instead of preventing them? Sometimes it's because prevention requires a very particular set of skills acquired over a long life. Also, prevention is messy and painful. You have to get close enough to know what each situation needs. And it's thankless. No one ever thanks you for preventing problems; just fixing them. Plus, prevention is more work upfront.

Prevention is crucial, though, as it mitigates complications, speeds rehabilitation, and improves quality of life. It also reduces risk factors, enables early detection, and manages the consequences of getting in and out of the ditch.

Gary can get you out of the ditch. Incredible counselors like AJ Molina (Founder of Master Peace Christian Counseling) provide hope to work through the ditch. People like Anna empathize while you're in the ditch. Each is part of the solution, but please don't neglect preventive care.

Many people rely on hospital emergency care. So too, many families rely on spiritual emergency care instead of preventive spiritual care. They stop the spiritual bleeding without removing the spiritual cancer. And that's no way to live. That's not the abundant life God intends for you. Here are five routines to help you prevent the chronic spiritual illnesses that occur in the lowest areas of your HEALTHY Home Wheel.

1. Get spiritual wellness checkups

I used to get "annual" physicals every five to ten years. It wasn't that I refused to go. I just didn't get around to it because I wasn't aware of any urgent problem.

Sadly, we often do the same spiritually. We need to know our spiritual condition, but we don't get around to it because we're unaware of any urgent problems. Spiritual wellness checkups can involve Christian counselors, accountability partners, small groups, godly mentors, and trusted online resources. Also, you can periodically update your HEALTHY Home Wheel to assess progress. Remember, you can't fix what you don't know, and you can't prevent what you don't think you need to know.

2. Shed your spiritual baggage

Obesity is a major cause of heart disease, strokes, diabetes, high blood pressure, aching joints, and more. You might be genetically prone to obesity, but that's a propensity, not an excuse. We all have propensities that become baggage unless we shed them. Otherwise, they become love handles that linger no matter how much weight we lose.

We also have spiritual propensities that we need to shed. Sure, it's hard to shed spiritual baggage, but you can do it. Randy Draper calls it: "Clean out your skeptic tank." Then again, spiritual baggage never smells great, but shedding it helps prevent the stink of chronic sins.

3. Release harmful stress

Good stress is a catalyst; bad stress, a burden. But since we can't avoid all bad stress, we must release it and refuse to return to it. Like the Old Testament kings who needed to cut down the idols in their land, we need to cut out the spiritual stressors and habits that endanger our spiritual health.

God tells us to cut out what enslaves and ensnares us (John 8:36, Prov. 5:22). Don't stew, harbor, or lash out. Release it. Put it behind you and press on (Phil. 3:12-14). Then there's room for the good stress that unleashes the best in you.

4. Follow God's prescriptions

When a friend had a stroke due to not taking his prescribed medicine, Anna got mad at me. So, why was I in trouble for his mistake? Because I had stopped taking my cholesterol medicine and she didn't want the same thing happening to me.

Similarly, by not following God's biblical prescriptions for spiritual health, we upset God and suffer the consequences. And we can't prevent chronic spiritual illness if we don't follow God's "big five" prescriptions of spiritual health – Bible, prayer, worship, fellowship, and witness.

5. Stay spiritually healthy together

The only way I stay healthy is when Anna and I do it together. It's not that we can't stay healthy on our own. We just don't unless we help each other. So too, committing to spiritual health with someone else is crucial. God designed us for community, so lean on your faith community to stay spiritually healthy together.

Staying fit also requires accountability. In our healthy lifestyles class, we had to text our weight every day to the leader. It's amazing how a little accountability drives healthier choices. A spiritual partner or mentor can also help you experience the third key to a healthy spiritual lifestyle – turning religion into an intimate, personal relationship with Jesus.

Relationship with Jesus

Turn religion into a relationship with Jesus

If you want a family that adores Jesus, *you* must adore Jesus. I call it "day-one passion" – living with the passion of a brand-new Christian. And the key to ongoing day-one passion is falling in love with Jesus all over again, like it's the first time. And that comes from an ever-deepening relationship with Him.

Jesus said the greatest commandment is to love God (Matt. 22:37). Thankfully, my kids were young when they chose to love God through saving faith. As a parent, that was THE goal – to get them into heaven. My faith had to become *theirs*. Deeply theirs. Here are three building blocks to help you and your family build a deeply personal relationship with God.

1.   A relationship built on God's love

With thousands of religions, the world isn't short on religion. But as noted earlier, every religion except Christianity tries to earn salvation. It's a sin built on our achievements, rather than on God's loving grace. If your relationship with Him reverts to just your works, you'll become like many European cathedrals I've visited – showy, but spiritually dead. The life is gone because the love is gone. Knowing about the God who died to save you isn't the same as abiding with Him.

For example, I would die to save my kids, but I'm far less likely to give my life for a stranger. Why? Because I don't love them in the same way as my kids.

But what I would never do is give my child's life to save a stranger, especially if they didn't appreciate the sacrifice. Hence, I can't fathom how God the Father could give His Son to die for us. But He did because He wants a relationship with us built on His agape love.

2. A relationship built on God's family

With so much talk in our society about "privilege," I realized that I'm privileged. Not because of skin color or financial status. As dirt-poor Mexican immigrants, my dad's family had nothing except a love of family and God. And that's why I'm privileged. I'm "spiritually privileged" because my family made it easy for me to be part of God's family. They taught me how to become a child of God, and their lives helped me want it for myself.

Is your family spiritually privileged because you make it easy for them to be part of God's family? Do you bear a striking resemblance to God, or do you treat God like a distant relative? Are you rooted and built in God (Col. 2:7), grafted into Him (Rom. 11:17), and growing in Him (John 15:1-7)? A great way to tell is by your service. Do you selflessly serve others, or do you selfishly expect them to serve you (Matt. 20:28)?

3. A relationship built on God's authenticity

Your family can trust God to be real if they can trust you to be real. They'll understand flaws, but they need you to be authentic. Credible. Reliable. True. Trustworthy. Consistent.

Authenticity was another quality I saw modeled as a kid. My parents were the same no matter where they were or who they were with. Dad didn't curse, scream, or tell dirty jokes at work or with friends because that wasn't his character. Mom didn't gossip or criticize, even in private, because she was the same person all the time. I may not have always agreed with them, but I always respected the fact that I knew what to expect from them – a loving, authentic relationship with them because they had a loving, authentic relationship with a loving, authentic God.

Authenticity has a special place in my family's heart too. For example, when each couple in my family picked their 26 A-to-Z character qualities (Chapter 8), they all chose authenticity as their "A" character quality. Although we're certainly not what we need to be, we are who we appear to be. And that's not an excuse for being who we want to be; it's a goal to emulate Jesus.

As we've seen, physical and spiritual health are similar. Physical health is the absence of illness and complete well-being, while spiritual health is the absence of ongoing sin and complete faithfulness.

Granted, you can't be 100% faithful on earth because you can never be 100% sin-free. But you can be 100% free. God can break the yokes and bonds that enslave you (Jer. 30:8). "If the Son sets you free, you will be free indeed" (John 8:36).

You no longer have to be a victim. You can be a victor in Christ. Perfect? No. But you can be perfectly complete in Him and experience complete freedom: "It is for freedom that Christ has set us free . . . (never) burdened again by a yoke of slavery" (Gal. 5:1).

Having an intimate relationship with Jesus is a glorious pursuit with a glorious promise: eternal life in heaven and vibrant life on earth. It's a blessed journey with a blessed destination. It's the life described at the funerals of my dear friends, Don O'Neal and Coy Moon, in Psalm 1:1-3:

> "Blessed is the one who does not walk in step with the wicked or stand in the way that sinners take or sit in the company of mockers, but whose delight is in the law of the LORD, and who meditates on his law day and night. That person is like a tree planted by streams of water, which yields its fruit in season and whose leaf does not wither – whatever they do prospers."

My prayer is that by practicing these big rocks and healthy habits, you won't live the spiritual version of my rollercoaster weight. I pray you'll build a strong spiritual metabolism and live with preventive spiritual care, not just emergency care. And if you revert to the spiritual chips of your old sin nature, I pray you'll reject your spiritual enemy and embrace the Savior who desperately wants an intimate relationship with you.

But that won't happen unless you determine to take the next steps of spiritual health.

Chapter 12

Take Next Steps to Spiritual Health

The older I get, the fewer things matter. But the few things that matter must truly matter *to me*. I have to embrace them and know how well I'm doing. Thus, this book started with the dream of spiritual health and assessing the spiritual health of you and your family.

Now that we've unpacked the 7 Big Rocks of spiritual health, please take a moment to update your preliminary HEALTHY Home Wheel scores from Chapter 2, which looked something like this for you (solid line) and your family (dotted line).

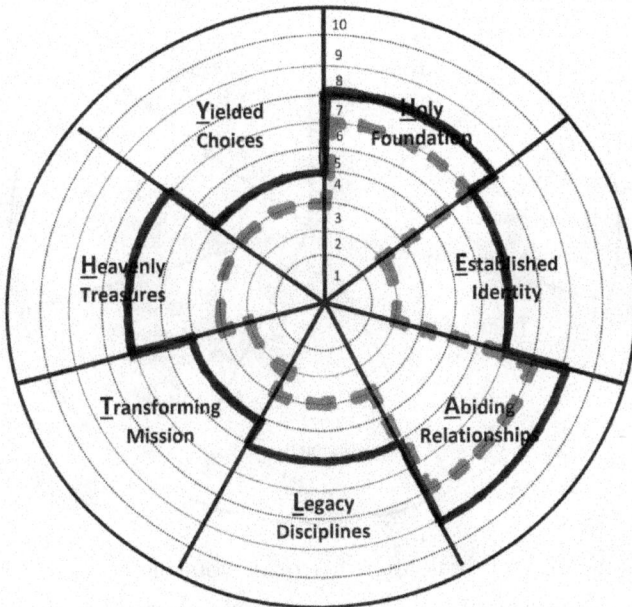

Please look back at your average scores for the 7 Big Rocks in Chapters 4 to 10 and write them below:

Your Updated 7 Big Rocks Scores:

	You	Home
Holy foundation	___	___
Established identity	___	___
Abiding relationships	___	___
Legacy disciplines	___	___
Transforming mission	___	___
Heavenly treasures	___	___
Yielded choices	___	___

Now, please chart your HEALTHY Home Wheel using these updated scores – a solid line for you and a dotted lines for your home.

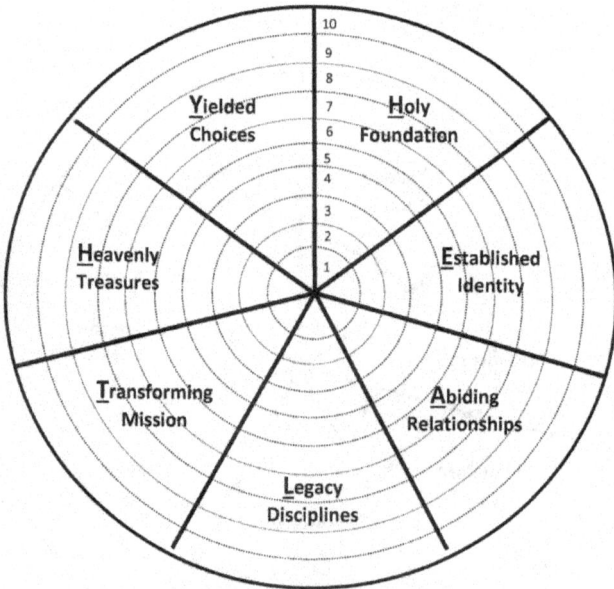

What do you think after re-scoring your big rocks? How did your preliminary scores change for you and your home? Which are the highest? The lowest? Which wheel is smoother – yours or your family's? Which wheel is larger? Which big rocks have the largest gaps between you and your family?

Similar to how each part of a house is vital for it to be successful, each big rock is vital for a home to be spiritually healthy. If any big rock is significantly low, you're weakening your family's opportunity to have a vibrant relationship with God. And since nothing is more important than your family's relationship with God, you can't afford any "tiny rocks." As I learned from my friend, Paul McCollum, here are five principles to turn those tiny rocks into spiritual boulders for God's glory.

1. Success principle: Bolster weaknesses and leverage strengths

Start with weaknesses because they're often all your family sees. For example, what do you see when a beautiful painting is covered in dirt? You see dirt, right? But when the dirt is removed, beauty is revealed. By removing your dirt, you'll help your family see how they can be world-changers, not just dirt-removers.

Next steps start with removing the dirt that muddies your strengths. But if a weakness doesn't distract, obsessing over it won't make you great. Bolstering weaknesses frees you up to be great by letting your strengths shine. So, if you want to change the world, focus more on your family's strengths than their faults.

2. Cap principle: Don't cap your family's health

If you want to predict your family's spiritual health, look at yours. Our HEALTHY home classes show that your home scores likely won't exceed yours because you're their cap. It's the same reason that work teams rarely rise above their leader. The leader is the cap. That's good news for your family and work team if you're a "9," but not if you're a "3." None of us want to be a cap, but we are unless, like Jabez, we ask God to enlarge the borders that limit us and our family (1 Chron. 4:9-10).

Which of your family's scores are lower than yours? Those are great places to take a next step because they're areas in which you can help your family improve.

3. Truth principle: Make God's Word your source of truth

Where do you get truth? No matter what society says, all "truth" is not true. "My truth" is a myth because truth is not subjective. Real truth is timeless and immutable because the only source of truth is God's Word – the Bible. But claiming the Bible is true isn't the same as making it your worldview. For when you see the world through the truth of the Creator, you can relate to everything He created (Col. 1:16).

The Bible is also the source of spiritual health. But as David Ingram puts it: "You have to get in it to live it." You have to know it, treasure it, and live it, not just hear it (James 1:22). And where can you start? Start with your updated HEALTHY Home Wheel, which reveals where God's truth needs to increasingly become the standard around which your life and home are built.

4. Grace principle: Give yourself the grace to be healthy

While we shouldn't think too highly of ourselves, we also shouldn't be our harshest critic. We must give ourselves the same thing God gives us – grace. We don't deserve unmerited favor, but we must give it to ourselves after we lay our sins at Jesus' feet and ask for His forgiveness.

If Satan can't get you with a lack of humility, He will try to defeat you with a lack of self-forgiveness. You may never be as spiritually healthy as you think you should be, but you can be clean in God's eyes through confession, repentance, and giving yourself the grace that He gives you.

5. Time principle: Give yourself the time to be healthy

The last principle for turning tiny rocks into spiritual boulders is also something few of us are good at – time, aka patience. I can't imagine what would happen if God wasn't patient with us. And what does God expect in return? Patience from us.

You may be patient with others, but are you patient with yourself? Do you give yourself the time needed to be spiritually healthy? Salvation occurs in an instant, but spiritual health marinates if you allow it to sink in.

Giving yourself time to grow isn't an excuse for poor habits; it's how you allow God to work in you so that He can work through you. But you have to start (or re-start) somewhere. So, start where you are, using the healthy habits you chose to be your next steps.

Where to take next steps

Please take a moment to summarize the healthy habits you picked to grow in Chapters 4 to 10. While improving all of the healthy habits from Ephesians is a great goal, a more realistic goal is to take practical next steps in specific areas that bring glory to God, draw you closer to Him, and help you walk worthy of your calling from Him (Eph. 4:1).

Holy foundation   _____

Established identity   _____

Abiding relationships   _____

Legacy disciplines   _____

Transforming mission   _____

Heavenly treasures   _____

Yielded choices   _____

How to take next steps

So, how do you break the process of spiritual health into doable parts? While you can use this book in many ways, I suggest splitting it up into nine parts: one session for your family dream and self-assessments (Chapters 1-3), seven sessions for the 7 Big Rocks of HEALHTY (Chapters 4-10), and one session to reassess your spiritual health and take action (Chapters 11-12).

But if you want to really dig in, consider covering the 7 Big Rocks over seven months or more. That allows time to break down each Big Rock into four weeks and discuss one of its four healthy habits and applications each week. For example, Anna and I will soon take part of our weekly date night to unpack one of the 28 healthy habits and how we want to become more like Christ in these 28 areas of spiritual health. The approach you take is up to you. Just choose one and go for it!

When to take next steps

The time to take next steps is now. Like my definition of success (maximize your opportunity and be faithful *today*), the only day in which you can be faithful is today. So, start or restart now.

And what about if you have kids or grandkids? I've found that we're quick to train kids in sports and music, but slow to train them in spiritual matters. We take them on vacation adventures, yet think it's too early to take them on spiritual adventures. Even if they don't yet grasp it all, start now with an age-appropriate approach. You'll reap the benefits of starting a bit early, but you'll lament the consequences of starting late.

With whom to take next steps

Although a healthy home starts with a healthy you, please don't do this by yourself. If you're married, pursue spiritual health with your spouse. If single, find a friend to join you. If you have kids, jump into the deep end of the pool and engage them in doing this together. Even though kids often act like they don't care, they'll later cherish the memories of growing spiritually together.

Another way to take next steps is mentoring. In Titus 2:3-8, Paul tells us to mentor younger people. So, why not help a mentee while you improve your own spiritual health? Mentoring isn't about having all the answers. It's about helping others in need of someone like you to join them in their spiritual journey.

Why to take next steps

Finally, please remember why building a spiritually healthy home is worth it. You're fulfilling your #1 ministry – helping your family want what they need to be faithful. Through "your good deeds (they) glorify your Father in heaven" (Matt. 5:16). As a steward of your family's eternity, though, you're not responsible for the results, just to walk worthy of your calling (Eph. 4:1).

There's nothing like the joy of seeing your family follow in your footsteps and, even better, surpass you spiritually. But even if your family members never become faithful, you can be faithful to do your part – preparing them to be spiritually healthy, not just happy. Yes, that's a big job, but you serve a big God who has big plans for your family. And you now have a guide with a framework and 7 Big Rocks upon which to take next steps.

A guide to take next steps

Over time, I've seen a scary trend – fewer and fewer people know the Bible and cling to its truth. So, they struggle with their spiritual identity and spiritual health. That's why I, along with David and Terry Ingram, created HEALTHY home classes for our church. And while many class attendees say it's helpful, they need more than a class to change their lives. They need a practical guide to help them navigate this journey.

That's what this book and a free Study Guide at timalba.com provide – a framework of spiritual health built on the Bible, practical truths, personal applications, and simple exercises. It's not intended to replace the Bible. It's designed to help the Bible become even more personal, powerful, and practical to each member of your family, starting with you.

And to guide you in implementing this framework of spiritual health, the next chapter provides discussion questions for each chapter to help you and your family/friends/mentees take next steps of spiritual health.

I pray that you'll accept this challenge and use this framework to turn the dream of a spiritually healthy family into a reality for *your* family. "May the grace of the Lord Jesus Christ, and the love of God, and the fellowship of the Holy Spirit be with you all" (2 Cor. 13:14). Godspeed!

Discussion Questions

Chapter 1   Choose a Family Spiritual Fitness Goal

1. Of the three Christian family dreams – happy home, holy home, or healthy home – which one are you, in reality, pursuing?

2. Which of these three dreams do you want to be your family's reality? Why?

3. How big is your family dream? What would help you aim more effectively at the target of a spiritually healthy family?

Chapter 2   Take a Spiritual Stress Test

1. What does this assessment say about the strength and consistency of your spiritual health and your home's spiritual health?

2. How wobbly is your own spiritual wheel? How does it affect your family and their wheels?

3. What big rocks are the strongest? Which ones need the most improvement and why?

Chapter 3   Build a HEALTHY Home

1. Which leadership style did you experience as a child – helped/ inspired, begged/coddled, or controlled/commanded? How does it still affect what you want as an adult? Which of these styles best describes how you lead your family?

2. How do your wants and needs get confused? How do you tend to confuse your family's needs with your own wants and needs? What would help you focus better on their needs?

3. To what degree is faithfulness the ultimate goal of your life and family leadership? So far, how would God describe your preparation of your family to be faithful?

Chapter 4   H – Holy Foundation

1.   What was your spiritual foundation as a child? How would your family describe their spiritual foundation, and how are you striving to build a holy foundation for them?

2.   Trinity: What does it say about God that He goes to such lengths to make you wholly holy? What does it say about your value? What does the Bible say about how God pursues you?

3.   Light-giver: How has God enlightened the eyes of your heart to know Him? And how has knowing God's boundless hope, rich inheritance, and incomparable power transformed your life?

4.   Savior: Do you ever find yourself trying to earn God's love instead of receiving it? How can you help your family take a next step in embracing His free gift of salvation through faith in Him?

5.   Creator: How does it feel to be set free, set apart, and set up to do Master-worthy works? How well do your good works reflect the fact that you're God's masterpiece?

Chapter 5   E – Established Identity

1.   Do your personal identity and your spiritual identity ever get confused? If so, how? What would strengthen your confidence in God's established identity for you – your spiritual floor plan?

2.   Adopted: How does it encourage you to know you can't be disowned as God's adopted child? Which do you value the most – God's love, God's acceptance, or God's stability, and why?

3.   Gifted: How has God gifted you to equip your family and His church? How could you help your family better know, embrace, and use their God-given gifts?

4.   Steward: How faithful have you been in stewarding your giftedness? If you met God right now in heaven, would He tell you, "Well done," or would it be something less?

5.   Temple: In what ways, if any, have you let Satan steal your spiritual identity? How could you take a next step in pursuing God and living more like who you are – His holy dwelling place?

Chapter 6   A – Abiding Relationships

1. How would He describe your relationship with Jesus Christ? How well are you and your family abiding in Him? What could you do to abide with Jesus like a vine abiding in its roots?

2. Submission: Who in your life models biblical submission? How do they live it? How would submitting, studying, and serving your family's needs grow you closer to God and each other?

3. Love-respect: Who needs your unconditional, undeserved love-respect, and how could you practically give it? How could you take a next step in emulating Jesus' example of love-respect?

4. Forgiveness: Who do you need to forgive? How could you go the extra mile to proactively pursue abundant mercy, grace, restoration, and joy in their lives?

5. Prayer: How does prayer act like duct tape to patch, fix, and seal frayed families and relationships? How have you seen God perform miracles through prayer?

Chapter 7   L – Legacy Disciplines

1. What "little" spiritual disciplines create big godly legacies? If you had better self-discipline to live with all these spiritual disciplines, how would they insulate your family from harm?

2. Humble conviction: Does your godly passion get imbalanced with too much humility or with too much confidence? How could a better balance prepare your family to absolutely adore Jesus?

3. Patience: If you ranked a list of your best qualities, where would patience be on that list? What would need to happen to make patience a strength of your family?

4. Unity: Does the way you handle conflict lead to family unity or discord? How could you help your family experience biblical unity and turn negatives into "wows!"?

5. Gratitude: For what blessings are you most thankful? For what difficulties do you struggle most to be grateful? How could you lead yourself and your family to be more grateful?

Chapter 8   T – Transforming Mission

1.   What's your family's unique God-given mission? What would your family say it is? If they can't articulate it, how can it enlighten their soul, capture their imagination, and transform their eternity?

2.   Success: What is your definition of success? Does it lead to faithfulness? Do you honor God by maximizing your opportunity and being faithful today with your God-given mission?

3.   Clarity: How clear and tangible is your mission? How can a mission transform your family if it's not transforming you? How would clarity improve your servant-leadership at home and work?

4.   Obedience: Do you tend to obey God wholeheartedly or compliantly? How have you disobeyed through delayed, partial, joyless, or conditional obedience?

5.   Missional: What won't you do to be more missional? What method won't you change? What definition or clarity won't you nail down? What commandment of God won't you obey?

Chapter 9   H – Heavenly Treasures

1.   What heavenly treasures – like spiritual décor – are filling your life and family? What stories do your spiritual treasures tell about what you value and what you'll lay at the feet of Jesus in heaven?

2.   Role model: Of whom would family say you're the spittin' spiritual image? Who in your life would you most like to emulate? What Bible person (other than Jesus) would it be, and why?

3.   Maturity: Are you more prone to powerless truth (truth without love) or misguided love (love without truth), and why? For whom could you begin to be an agent of spiritual maturity?

4.   Generosity: What examples of overflowing generosity have you received or given? What would need to change for you to be able to give the treasure of generosity to Jesus?

5.   Resilience: How stubborn are you with God's standard of faithfulness? How willing and able are you to be trustworthy and trust God . . . to do your part and trust God to do His?

Chapter 10   Y – Yielded Choices

1.   Which kinds of choices define you – determined choices or default choices? What healthy choices help you (or people you admire) yield to God's will and protect your family?

2.   Choose: How consistently do you wear God's armor? Which pieces of His armor are hardest to put on every day? How has Satan attacked the pieces of God's armor that you didn't put on?

3.   Pre-choose: Why is it so important to pre-choose boundaries of purity? What are some of the most crucial lines of compromise that you can't afford to cross or even get close?

4.   Un-choose: What parts of your old sin nature do you most need to keep un-choosing? What changes would help you put off the old sinful you and put on the new you in Christ?

5.   Re-choose: What next steps would help you proactively let the Holy Spirit fill you? More than a plan to follow, how could you more consistently follow God's plan for you and your family?

Chapter 11   Live a Spiritually Healthy Lifestyle

1.   In what ways has your physical health mirrored your spiritual health? How has your spiritual health been a rollercoaster of highs and lows? How could fewer lows help your family?

2.   Spiritual metabolism: How could you increase your spiritual metabolism? To what degree do you drink enough spiritual water, consume balanced spiritual meals, strengthen your spiritual core, exercise your spiritual gifts, and rest for spiritual well-being?

3.   Preventive spiritual care: Do you tend to live with spiritual emergency care or preventive spiritual care, and why? How could you benefit by investing more in preventive spiritual care?

4.   Relationship with Jesus: How would God describe your relationship with Him? On what have you built your relationship with God, and what would significantly deepen that relationship?

Chapter 12   Take Next Steps to Spiritual Health

1.   After rescoring the 7 Big Rocks of a HEALTHY home, how did your initial scores change? What did you learn about you and your home? What next steps can you take to grow?

2.   Which of the 7 Big Rocks are your biggest strengths? Your biggest weaknesses?

3.   Which of the 7 Big Rocks have the biggest gaps between you and your family, and why?

4.   How would smoothing your spiritual wobble improve your family's life and eternity?

5.   How would enlarging your spiritual wheel improve your family's life and eternity?

Your Next Steps

A free *HEALTHY Home* Study Guide, along with other spiritual health resources, are available at www.TimAlba.com. Print as many copies of that online Study Guide as needed for your family, Bible study group, mentees, or any other group that wants a spiritually healthy home for themselves and people they love.

Get Tim's free blogs by signing up at www.TimAlba.com/blog. You'll receive inspirational content on topics like parenting, home/career leadership, character, faith, and family.

For another resource to help your family be faithful, get your copy of Tim's first book, *Well Done, Mom & Dad!, A Practical Guide to Turn Good Intentions into Godly Legacies*. It was called "mandatory reading for every Christian parent" by Jim Burns, President of HomeWord Ministries.

For free personal coaching or to have Tim speak at an event, please contact him at:

TimAlbaWD@gmail.com
www.TimAlba.com

Dedication

This book is dedicated to my bride, Anna. Our kids exude spiritual health because they see it so consistently in you. You're always loving and gracious. Always serving and joyful. Always the glue that binds our family together.

Many people made *HEALTHY Home* possible, especially John Meador (my pastor and dear friend, who developed a sermon series based on this book), David and Terry Ingram (my co-teachers of HEALTHY home classes), Sharon Smith (my editor and inspiring role model), Josh Merriott (my Barnabas, who helped flesh out the house analogy), and my parents and sister (who consistently model it).

The most important dedication, though, goes to Jesus Christ – my rock and fortress. Although I never planned to write this book, it was a privilege to do so because You showed me the need, revealed this framework from Ephesians, and infused a renewed joy in my soul. Thank You, Lord, for loving me and giving me the privilege of being Your child.

About the Author

As a husband, dad, financial executive, and former executive pastor, Tim Alba has a unique ability to apply biblically-based success principles learned at both home and work. This book and his first book, *Well Done, Mom & Dad!,* are the culmination of a lifelong pursuit of Tim's passion: to hear God say, "Well done!" and help others do the same.

Tim's story is one of simple obedience. When God called Tim to surrender his role as CFO and part-owner of CiCi's Pizza to serve his church full-time, he obeyed wholeheartedly. Eight years later, when God led him to leave his pastoral role, Tim found new ministry opportunities at work, church, and as an author.

His family leadership was featured in *Stories of True Financial Freedom: God's Impact in Real Lives* by Crown Financial Ministries. And his work leadership was featured in *Your Signature Work: Creating Excellence and Influencing Others at Work* by Dianna Booher.

Tim and his wife, Anna, serve families through small group classes, www.timalba.com, free personal coaching, and seminars near their home in the Dallas/Fort Worth area. They have three kids, three "bonus" kids (their kids' spouses), and six grandkids.

Ephesians Verses

Ephesians 1
1:4 Trinity (H)
1:5 Adopted (E)
1:7-8 Generosity (H)*
1:18-19 Light-giver (H)

Ephesians 2
2:8-9 Savior (H)
2:10 Creator (H)
2:21-22 Temple (E)

Ephesians 3
3:2 Steward (E)
3:9 Clarity (T)
3:12 Humble conviction (L)
3:17-19 Missional (T)
3:20 Generosity (H)*
3:32 Forgiveness (A)

Ephesians 4
4:1 Success (T)
4:2a Humble conviction (L)
4:2b Patience (L)
4:3-4 Unity (L)
4:7 Gifted (E)
4:11-13 Gifted (E)
4:14-15 Maturity (H)*
4:22-24 Un-choose (Y)
4:32 Forgiveness (A)

Ephesians 5
5:1 Role model (H)*
5:3 Pre-choose (Y)
5:11-12 Pre-choose (Y)
5:16 Success (T)
5:17 Obedience (T)
5:18 Re-choose (Y)
5:20 Gratitude (L)
5:21 Submission (A)
5:33 Love-respect (A)

Ephesians 6
6:6-8 Obedience (T)
6:10 Resilience (H)*
6:13-17 Choose (Y)
6:18 Prayer (A)

Note: (H) is Holy foundation. (H)* is Heavenly treasures.

* 9 7 8 1 9 4 1 5 5 5 6 2 0 *